This & That

Part 1

by

Irene Kellar Mueller

Published by Connection Publications

Connection Publications
P.O. Box 55
Greenbank, WA 98253

First Edition

Library of Congress Catalog Card Number: 98-96904

ISBN 0-9668980-0-1

Printed in the United States

Cover by Bartelson Designs
105 S Main
Coupeville, WA 98239

Cover photograph by Irene Kellar Mueller

- - Dedicated To Many - -

Rilla Ertresvaag
Gordie for his patience
Shellie, Valerie, Beckie, Rick and Gary who said I could
Derold, Dona, Bev and Lois who said I should
Jenny who gave me the time so I would
The Coupeville Examiner editor Keven for smoothing the edges
The people of Central Whidbey Island for their trust

Longtime Islander keeps Madrona Way picturesque

July 12, 1996

Our Central Whidbey community loves music and beauty. In both, we are a divided people. There are those who sing, play an instrument or dance and those who just enjoy listening and watching as others do. In the beauty area, there are those who toss trash and those who pick it up. Lillian Huffstetler picks it up.

Since 1949, Lillian has kept Madrona Way clean and neat between the yearly visits from the local Lions. "If I'm going to get my exercise," she says, "I might as well do something good instead of just sitting on a machine." And she does.

She can be found early in the morning with her little pick-up stick removing debris from the lagoon to the beach railing. She has found that many people finish their fast food about the time they hit Madrona Way. And that's where the boxes and bags are discarded.

"If people didn't eat, drink or smoke in their cars, there wouldn't be a problem," Lillian said. The cigarette butts worry her most. The dry pine needles are just ripe for a fire. Her strangest find was the paraffin from a jar of jelly. "Who opens jelly jars driving down the road?" she asked.

Lillian wishes people would drive slower on Madrona Way and can't believe it when tourists stop in the middle of the road to enjoy the view.

Once in a while, people honk or give her a thumbs up, and she enjoys that. Thank you, Lillian.

***

Sunday's Buellgrass concert at the Coupeville Recreation Hall was a sell-out with an audience of all ages, said Elkhorn Trading Co.'s Julie Lloyd. "Top of the line," Vern Olsen said, "unreal."

***

A few Mondays ago in Teronda West, lawn mowers were turned off, kids stopped shouting and builders stopped their hammers as the Shifty Sailors practiced on Gordie and Irene Mueller's deck.

The only sounds were of the waves slapping the beach below and the 13 men singing to their hearts' content.

Led by Vern Olsen, they laughed a lot, changed a key or two and serenaded the neighborhood with *One More Day*, *Shenandoah*, and a dozen other favorites.

The Shifty Sailors first sang as a group in December 1993 in celebration of the release of the Island County Historical Society Book and the Museum display, *Sails, Steamships and Sea Captains*.

Fishing duo land $2,500 prize

July 19, 1996

Bob Watt and Virgil Blanton almost missed the Island Adventure/ Fenwick Salmon Derby in Anacortes. They heard about the two-day event just before the deadline. The partners paid the $200 entry fee and went out to try their luck in Bob's 19 foot New Bay Osprey.

By 2 p.m. the first day, they had reeled in what they hoped was a winner, a 24.46 pound king salmon. They held their breath until the final weigh-in on Sunday.

A 30 pound king was caught, but the fisherman hadn't registered for the derby, so Bob and Virgil walked away with decals, a trophy and $2,500 to split between them.

Bob lives in Coupeville with his wife Janice who works at Prairie Center. Janice worked the weekend and missed all the excitement. Virgil lives in Oak Harbor.

The Derby will be held again next year, and Bob and Virgil will be there. And since half of $2,500 didn't bring retirement, they were back to work at Brown & Root at the Navy base on Monday.

Congratulations!

***

Bob and Judi Davis, of Coupeville's Davis and Davis Inc., leave next week for Bucerias, Mexico where they will make their home during the winter months.

In June, they'll be back for the summer after grandsons Joshua and Jacob finish the 1996-1997 school year in Mexico.

Bob and Judi have both contributed much to our community, especially to Concerts on the Cove and Coupeville Arts Center.

They will be missed.

***

The All American Boys Chorus is scheduled to perform in Coupeville Friday, August 16. Housing is needed for the members for two nights.

If you can host some of these talented artists, call 678-4684.

***

Did you know that Coupe's Greenbank Store is open 7 days a week from 7 a.m. to 9 p.m. ?

Well stocked, nice people.

Teas ease transition for school chief's daughter

July 26, 1996

Entertaining is fun for Jan and Marshall Bronson. They invite large groups into their home, The Compass Rose Bed and Breakfast, for a great variety of parties.

And Jan is no stranger to tea parties. She says she attended at least three a week at their last duty assignment in Montevideo, Uruguay where Marshall was Naval and Defense Attaché at the American Embassy. They have lived all over the world and know moving can be hard, even for adults.

Jan also knows moving to a new school can be painful for a child of any age. So she and Marshall gave 9-year-old Cavan a golden chance to meet new friends.

Cavan is the daughter of Suzanne Bond, the new superintendent of Coupeville schools.

Cavan was guest of honor at two tea parties at The Compass Rose. A total of 15 young ladies dressed in their best, came to meet Cavan. The girls shared tiny sandwiches, Boston cookies, and scones with raspberry jam, prepared by the Captain himself.

Serving as junior hostess at the second tea party was Megan, the bronzed California niece of Herb and Susan McDonald.

The first day of school could have been difficult for Cavan. Now, thanks to the Bronsons, it will undoubtedly be much easier.

***

On July 10, Jan and Marshall celebrated their 4th anniversary as owners of The Compass Rose Bed & Breakfast on South Main.

Jan says owning a B&B is "more fun than I thought it would be, the guests are more charming and the work load is greater than I ever dreamed it could be."

Drive by their B&B. Roses are peeking over the top of their new picket fence. It's a picture out of a story book.

***

***

I hope "it could only happen on Whidbey Island" extends to Longview.

Dona and Greg Forney and children Seth, Jed, Kalynn, and Shiloe moved there this week.

We all have people in our lives who are more family than friends. The Forneys, for us, were just that.

Shiloe was just a little guy when they moved here. More than once, I was surprised to find him peeking around my desk or tiptoeing down the hall where, he said, he was "just lookin."

Never did know what he was "lookin" for.

Kalynn followed me around the yard, helping when she could and talking about her day at school.

And Jed. Jed and my grandson spent hours together playing on the organ, fixing hot chocolate in my kitchen or skate boarding down the street.

The Forneys have the kind of kids I wish I'd had time to raise.

Sundays were always family day. No one intruded on their one day together.

It was beautiful, and the kids loved it.

Surely there must be someone in Longview who cares about people exactly the way Whidbey Islanders do.

Maybe they'll meet someone like the Bronsons in their new town.

***

Drive out on Engle Road and you will find a huge field of mixed sweet peas. Smells like heaven.

***

Did you see the sunset Sunday evening. Did you take time to enjoy it?

***

Happy Birthday Mary Jo Isenmann!

Chamber's Ary joins 'don't let it happen to you' club

August 2, 1996

Marie Ary, Director of Central Whidbey Chamber of Commerce, says she could be the poster child for the "don't let it happen to you" club.

Driving to the chamber meeting one Monday morning, Marie tried to shoo an insect out of her car, lost control and landed in the ditch.

She spent the night at Whidbey General with a concussion and went home with her left hand in a splint.

She can do some work from her home, but Rita Kuller, owner of Rita's Rainbow next to the CWCC Visitor's Center on North Main Street, has been taking care of many of Marie's chamber duties.

Marie and husband Ben, a design engineer for Boeing, have lived in Coupeville since December. They love the friendliness, the pace of life, and are delighted to be where people give so much time to the community.

Marie started working for the chamber in March and has it down pat. She's doing a great newsletter, organized a fine Memorial Day Parade, and has the Visitor's Center running smoothly.

Good job, Marie!

***

Speaking of Central Whidbey Chamber of Commerce.

The community owes a debt of gratitude to Sandy Roberts for his steadfast support of local businesses. Back when Windermere Real Estate\Center Isle was Center Isle Realty, owner Sandy Roberts offered the services of his company personnel to the chamber.

Although all members of Roberts' staff helped, Jacquie Kellems (now Vincent) did the bulk of the work until she retired in 1992. In the May, 1991 chamber newsletter, Jacquie said, "CIR has been answering the phone, handing out literature and mailing tourist and relocation packets for CWCC for six plus years."

That's since 1985!

Every month, she sent the number of calls and requests CIR had answered to me and I printed them in the CWCC newsletter.

In her last monthly report, 304 requests had been responded to by the 14 staff members.

That took a lot of time from real estate sales!

Not only did Roberts give the time of his personnel to the chamber, he also served on the board. Back then, he was chairman of both Business Development and New Business Promotion and played an important role on many other committees.

And Roberts is still giving.

Today, Sandy Shields at Windermere Real Estate/Center Isle takes over 30 calls a day from all over the United States. Questions range from "when is low tide on Friday?" to "how can I reach the wood shop across from the post office?"

Every time a potential tourist/customer gets the right answer, the whole community wins.

Next time you see Sandy Roberts, tell him you know what he's doing!

***

I know we have to have safe roads, but every time I drive past the intersection of State Highway 20 and Highway 525 where so many trees are being removed to widen the road, my heart hurts.

***

Heat doesn't hinder Hancocks' Texas trek

August 9, 1996

Texas in July may seem impossible to some of us, but not to the Hancocks. Alan, Elizabeth, Emily and Benjamin found the hot, humid temperature very comfortable.

"Everything was air conditioned - - cars, motels, shops, "outside," they said, "everything was green."

The two-week, 2,800 mile journey was "the very best vacation ever" Elizabeth said, a "neat trip with no problems."

It's important to enjoy the local food on any trip, and the Hancocks did. They *ate it all* — Cajun, huge Texas barbecues, and in Galveston, catfish and crawfish etouffee.

The Hancocks visited the space shuttle tracking station at NASA, toured LBJ's ranch west of Austin, rode a tour boat down the canal beside the "River Walk" in San Antonio and visited the Alamo and the San Jacinto Battlefield Monument northeast of Houston.

Sadly, a very small part of the Texas battlefields are preserved and the area is surrounded by active chemical plants. Chemical plants are everywhere in Louisiana, too. Only a few acres of plantation lands are untouched.

Highlight was a visit to Shirley Mae, Elizabeth's 86-year-old cousin, twice removed. Shirley Mae's New Orleans home has gold framed portraits of her (and Elizabeth's) ancestors. She and her daughters all reigned as Mardi Gras queens and their pictures also graced the walls.

Last time the Hancocks visited Shirley Mae and her late husband Beep, they did all the clubs. Not this time. They found Bourbon Street interesting, but skipped the night life.

Baseball fans, the Hancocks drove to Arlington Stadium out of Dallas for the July 18 game. Imagine watching the Rangers play the Oakland 'A's and staying calm while keeping an eye on the scoreboard over on the sidelines showing the Mariners whipping the Angels in California.

Yes!

***

You could win a 6X8 storage shed for $1!

Offered by the Central Whidbey Lions Club, the drawing is Sunday, August 11 at the arts and crafts festival. Proceeds go to the Community Service Fund.

The Lions do a lot of good works. Let's support them!

***

Housing is still needed for the young singers for the Concerts on the Cove sponsored All American Boys Chorus on August 16.

Call Susan McDonald, 678-4540 if you have an extra bed or two.

***

Vivian and Bill Carboneau and son Rob are home after kayaking along the east side of the DNR Park on Lummi Island. Starting from Hale Spit, they found beauty and privacy.

Viv did a solo on the 8-mile trip back down. She won't do that again for a while.

***

Peggy Arnold sent starter batter for her Amish Friendship Bread. Takes a lot of squeezing of the bag, but the finished product is delicious.

Great therapy.

***

After you visit all the shops in Coupeville, try Freeland. Shop after shop chock-full of wonderful things.

If you can't find what you want, Sonya Ross at Whidbey Trader's, Inc., will help. Tell her Irene sent you.

***

Whidbey Island captures San Antonio couple

August 16, 1996

Bob and Shirley Erb lived in San Antonio for 57 years, came to our town on a Thursday, fell in love with Whidbey Island, bought land on Saturday and went home on Sunday to pack. They're back, living in a house they rented sight unseen and loving the view, the weather, and until their pots and pans arrive, the Tyee Cafe. Welcome!

***

Need something fun to do on Saturday nights? Late Nite Central may be the answer. Help oversee the activities when Coupeville students in grades six through nine gather at the school for an evening with their friends from 7:30-10:30 p.m. .

Janet Wodjenski says it's a wonderful opportunity to get to know our kids. "No, they don't look like you and I did at their age, and sometimes that's scary. But when you see them playing board games, basketball, badminton or volleyball, or just hanging out, they are much the same."

Table tennis pro Hank Toucher volunteers regularly and teaches the game to anyone who wants to learn.

Late Nite Central has a wish list: complete board games, a boom box, and a functional refrigerator. They are sharing a fridge with the Coupeville Booster Club that's not so good.

Late Night Central was created following a drug and alcohol survey in the Coupeville schools. A group of parents formed the Radical Pack which eventually became The Youth Coalition.

Radical Pack says it all: "*R*ally *A*gainst *D*rugs *I*n our *C*ommunity *A*nd our *L*ives. *P*ublic *A*wareness for *C*oupeville *K*ids."

The goal is to offer after hours activities to students. Carmen McFadyen conducted a successful trial run of Late Night Central in 1994 and the program began.

During the school year about 40 kids show up. The number dwindles during the summer, but there is a core group that always comes to play basketball or just be with friends.

Except for August 24, Late Night Central is open every Saturday.

To volunteer, call Director Christy Chapman at 678-1927.

***

Ed and Mary Ellen Puck celebrated their 50th wedding anniversary with family and friends Saturday.

Ed retired in 1976 from Everett Community College where he taught physical education before switching to administration to work in student activities during the 1960s. Mary Ellen says she remembers well those rebellious years.

Residents of Central Whidbey for 18 years, the Pucks have two children and one grandchild.

Ed loves his golf and is a regular at Whidbey Golf and Country Club. Mary Ellen, who has volunteered "since the beginning of time," now limits herself to one day a week at the Island County Historical Society Museum where she has served for seven years.

Congratulations!

***

The arts and crafts booths were calling us, but our 5-year old twin grandchildren, Jason and Jordie, remembered last year and knew just where to go Saturday. Before anything else, we had to "do" the kids activities in Town Park!

They were right.

Little artists were praised for their efforts and enjoyed the patience and encouragement of the volunteers.

Activity chairman Debbie Sherman's workers never stopped smiling as they folded and glued reams of tissue, rescued tipped over containers of sparklers, and calmed youngsters eagerly waiting their turn to create.

And they did create.They decorated sea shells, personally designed wind socks, one of a kind hand stamped kerchiefs.

Once again the Arts & Crafts Festival Committee presented us with a wonderful event. Thank you all!

1997, same time, same place.

***

Every word Kathy Sechrist wrote in her letter to the editor last week is true. I just stopped too soon. I haven't forgotten the enthusiasm and dedication Kathy and crew brought to our community. As the new CIR/Windermere office manager, Kathy expanded their eight page quarterly newsletter to 12 pages, a wealth of information. And Kathy did indeed compile the chamber statistics after Jacquie Vincent retired.

***

Don't miss The All American Boys Chorus 7 p.m. Friday in the Coupeville Performing Arts Center.

Youth sports helping build kids self-esteem

August 23, 1996

John Schisel was "scared spitless" when he started coaching soccer five years ago.

Thanks to experienced coaches who steered him through the hard times, he now enjoys the job and serves as soccer director for CWYAA, Central Whidbey Youth Athletic Association, a non-profit, all volunteer organization, sponsored by local businesses.

John's company, Schisel Construction, one of the sponsors, has been in business on the island for eight years. He just completed the new building on Front Street. John also chairs the Artists in Action division of the Coupeville Arts & Crafts Festival.

John didn't get into sports as a child in New Jersey. He wasn't a *good* player and being a *little* guy, he felt he didn't have a lot to offer any team.

That's what he sees today in too many kids. Low self esteem, lack of confidence, and worried about playing a sport they know nothing about.

Once they get started, he says, they love it. Good coaches make all the difference. John could use a few. He's not looking for 'great' coaches. He says the requirements are liking kids, being sensitive to their self esteem, and having a good sense of humor.

Two hundred boys and girls, from kindergarten through grade ninth grade want to play soccer this year. You can make it happen.

Call John 678-3691.

***

Recently, we attended an educational safari at the beautiful Olympic Park Institute on Lake Crescent. Stuffed sandwiches in our backpacks and hiked with 59 other grandparents and grandkids for what seemed like an eternity.

Enjoyed the rain forest, the falls, and Hurricane Ridge and will be forever grateful for an afternoon of soaking in the Sol Duc Hot Springs.

It's true. Some human beings are more "fit" than others.

***

***

Heidi Hennessey and Simon Bargh have been running Rosi's Garden Restaurant since June and will become the new owners next week.

Heidi is the daughter of Al and Marion Sasso, owners of The Victorian Bed & Breakfast, and for a bit longer, Rosi's.

Originally from New York, Heidi has lived in Washington eight years. She knows the restaurant business. Her dad and two brothers are chefs and she has worked in all areas of the business for 15 years.

Simon, a chef for eight years, specializes in sea food preparation.

Since local Bed and Breakfast owners recommend Rosi's Garden Restaurant to their guests, Heidi and Simon sent an open invitation to those owners to come to Rosi's for a dinner on the house.

The invitation gives Heidi and Simon an opportunity to meet the owners and to thank them for sending business their way.

Seafood is the choice of most of Rosi's guests with an osso buco you can cut with a fork, a close second.

The restaurant has been famous for its prime rib since Michael, the original owner, opened and it continues to be a favorite.

Welcome and congratulations to Coupeville's newest business owners.

***

Did you know: It takes 20 positive statements to offset one negative remark hurled in anger?

Children are particularly sensitive. They trust parents and other adults to tell the truth.

If you tell a child he is dumb, he believes you.

It can take a lifetime to erase the pain.

***

Rediscover island by playing tourist

August 30, 1996

Want to experience a real eye-opener?

Play tourist with someone who has never been to Whidbey Island.

After a reunion in Seattle, my Missouri sister Dona, and her girls came home with us. Dona had been here, the girls hadn't. On the ferry, we rode with them out on the "wings" where the tourists stand, and watched the island come closer and closer.

It's been a long time since we noticed the houses sitting right on the edge of the water, their windsocks flying in the breeze.

Driving up the island, the phone booth on Classic Road delighted our guests. And Bonnie, a Realtor, thought Leona's "Loganberry Realty" sounded like a wonderful place to work.

As we turned onto our road, the Puget Sound stretched before us, and seeing the beauty, Brenda almost drove into the ditch.

I remembered feeling that way when I made that turn a long, long time ago. Now it's just a road taking me home.

Once in our driveway, our guests were out of the car and up on the deck in an instant to see if they had imagined the magnificence. They were in awe of the "diamonds" sparkling on the water, the ships, and the sight of Port Townsend, the ferries, the lighthouse.

Two seals were playing below us and just when we thought the show was over, the sun dropped and colored the sky from pink to bright orange and set oh, so slowly. As if it hated to go.

And when the stars came out, we were still sitting on the deck.

Monday, we picked blackberries during our walks through the woods and down to the beach. The colors and shapes of the rocks on the beach fascinated us once again. For ages, we've only gone down for fireworks on the 4th of July.

And we went shopping in Coupeville. Yes, the shops are open on Monday, and they are full of items beautifully displayed. Our guests were amazed at the uniqueness of Front Street, the historical B&B's, the flower boxes on the sidewalks and the size and quality of our Museum.

Seeing a deer calmly standing by the road, beautiful Puget Sound, the beach, and our town through our visitors' eyes, I promised myself I will never again become so busy or blasé that I don't enjoy the beauty of our world.

Try the tourist trip - - it is indeed an eye-opener!

***

Happy Birthday, Shellie Mandell and Jenny Grant!

Former town mayor declared kite king

September 6, 1996

For the last 6 years, during the fourth week of August, Jane and Will Jones have been in Long Beach, Washington where Will competes in the International Kite Festival .

This year, he came home with two Blue Ribbons!

Will entered two 100 kite-trains, an Eddy and an Ohashi, in the competition and took First Prize for his 100 Eddy Kite-train.

He also won a Special 1st Prize Award for his custom designed kite carriers. Shaped like his kites, the carriers are on wheels and make toting and setting up easier.

"This is Will's hobby and he does it all totally on his own," Jane said.

He studies kite catalogs from all over the country for the perfect rip-stop nylon in just the right color tones. With the brilliant colored material spread on the floor, a color chart is used to choose the arrangement and design of the tails.

Jane's only job during the planning stage, is to help with the color wheel. Will makes the final decisions.

And he does all the work.

Using a second hand Bernina, he sews and constructs his kites over a period of about a year.

"Judges at the International Kite Festival look at *everything*," Jane said, "The colors, their shape and arrangement, and at every stitch."

Will, former mayor of Coupeville, became interested in his hobby in 1984 and attends classes in the art at Fort Warden and Long Beach several times a year. He practices at Camp Casey now and then, but the winds here are "pretty gusty."

Jane also attends the classes in Long Beach, but her involvement is limited. During the competition, she keeps the Jones' supplied with hamburgers and helps get the kites up.

This year, she had one more job.

Will was out in the field and didn't hear his name announced as the winner. She had to give him the word.

Congratulations to the Blue Ribbon Winner!

***

***

Ruth Gonhue set aside the 11 quarts of beans she canned today and told me she is "85 years old and running out of steam."

So we talked about that steam.

Again this year, Ruth co-chaired the Methodist Strawberry Festival which she says is a "big eating deal." She is also involved in the women's luncheons at the church, and after 23 years, continues to help serve weekly dinners to the Coupeville Lions. She visits the sick and elderly at Whidbey General and at Careage regularly, often taking them bouquets left from the church service.

Recently, Ruth cleaned out a berry patch for her 92-year-old friend who needed help.

Active Methodists, Ruth and her husband Wes transferred membership from Marysville to Coupeville when they moved here in 1973. Until his death in 1995, they worked together in church activities.

They were there every day when the church was remodeled. "We were kinda' the clean up crew," Ruth said. "Wes dug ditches and I was in charge of the volunteers and arranged for snacks and coffee for the workers."

Raised on a farm in Marysville, Ruth graduated from high school in 1928, and started teaching in a one room school house in 1930. During summers, she attended Bellingham Normal, (now Western Washington State University) to earn her Teacher's Life Certificate.

"No one could teach with a Life Certificate today," she says, "but I did a good job."

The state didn't accept married teachers then, so, after she and Wes married in 1937, she was only allowed to substitute. The rules changed in the early '40s and she went back to work. Ruth taught for 30 years - - 23 of those years in intermediate grades, then 7 years of steady substituting.

She still lives near Coupeville on the beach property they bought from an uncle 59 years ago "when it was cheap." They built a weekend cabin on the property and still use it when necessary.

The 11 quarts of beans she canned?

They came from the garden she and Irene Wanamaker grow together. They think they might "call it quits this year, but," Ruth laughed, "we'll see."

Running out of steam? I don't think so.

Kon-Tiki 'a statement' about her home

September 13, 1996

No, Coupeville's Kon-Tiki is not a restaurant, nor a business, says Linda Sharp, "It's a statement about my home and how I relate to the sea, the beginning of everything."

Sailing ships didn't start from Coupeville, she said. Sea captains on sailing ships found Coupeville. "As I did." Sailors know where the wind and currents will take them, "and they brought me here."

"I'm not Dutch, I'm not a farmer, I'm a skipper, and I live by the water in a house of Scandinavian architecture." And it was a Scandinavian, she explained, who led the Kon-Tiki expedition in 1947 and later wrote a book about the voyage.

Ergo, the name on her home, she said. "It's no different than putting a name on a boat. It's a part of me."

The entry to her home speaks to her other passion, painting. Richly painted panels of fired enamel on steel line the outside of the home, each telling a story. The panels, for 20 years, were part of a mural outside the Hotel Sheraton in Portland.

Linda knew the artist who did the panels and the Kon-Tiki lettering. She acquired them when the Sheraton became the Marriott and has stored the art for 17 years.

A Washington native, Sharp has always lived by the water. A skipper since 1977, she owns the Quinault Lady II, has raced on the Columbia River and was a crew member in the Whidbey Island Races and the Women's Adams Cup.

Linda bought her home on Parker Road two years ago, but didn't meet anyone until she installed the lettering. "Something else really good has come of this," she said. "Kids stop by to ask what Kon-Tiki means and I send them off to the library. When kids read, they learn."

Kon -Tiki, the book, is available at the Coupeville Library and Thor Heyerdahl's autobiography can be ordered.

Pick them up, they're fascinating.

***

Tara Carboneau and Jim Gullett were married at The Old Morris Farm Bed & Breakfast on Saturday, Sept. 7, 1996. Congratulations!

***

Happy Birthday to Rita Kuller of Rita's Rainbow Thrift and Gift Shop on North Main Street.

***

Caroline King, owner of *Of Course* on Grace Street, knows what she's talking about when she advises "use it while you've got it."

Recovering from a broken wrist and dislocated left hand she sustained in a fall in July, Caroline appreciates, even more than before, the problems of those who are less fortunate than she.

Even as a child she had empathy for the handicapped. She once went blindfolded for a week learning to "see" with her ears.

It was an opportunity to experience what a blind person lives with daily.

"You can see a lot of things with your ears," she said, adding "it's the same thing now, I've learned to cope."

Her hand has 'no oomph,' she says, and insists that after being in a cast for six weeks, "it's been on vacation too long - - it's time to wake up and get going!"

Caroline has become very creative in completing projects. She's learned to use her knees to hold pillow slips and her teeth to hold scraps of cotton to finish crib bumper pads for an October baby.

"I've always been accident prone, with at least one boo-boo every year," she said.

Her husband, Don, has been gracious most of the time, but she hopes "he never comes back as a woman — it would be a real disaster." Don helps put her combs in her hair, a simple process for her, she said, but for him, impossible.

There is an upside. Caroline's had time to do what she really likes to do - - write poetry. She said she doesn't worry about forgetting her poetic thoughts during her work day. She has the ability to lock ideas in her head like a tape as she thinks of them. Problem: sometimes she finds she's running on a half dozen different tapes at one time.

Feeling better now that the cast is off and her hand is on the mend, Caroline is grateful for her customer's patience and understanding.

A speedy, full recovery, Caroline!

***

Lillian Huffstetler had heart surgery September 4. She is home and being cared for by her friends, Winnie Shelton and Vivian Fisher.

Lillian was featured in the July 12, 1996 issue for her service to our community.

Best wishes, Lillian!

Bidding a sad farewell to Gudmunson family

September 20, 1996

Jerilee Gudmunson is one busy lady.

Her husband David, stationed aboard the USS Abraham Lincoln in Bremerton, comes home weekends and whenever he can during the week, but their three active children, Ryan 15, Aaron 13, and Jenna 11, are pretty much her job. She makes the whole thing seem easy.

"Everything is fun — life is fun!" she said.

That's how she makes it all happen.

Jerilee volunteers at the school for field trips - - loved the eight mile hike to Fort Ebey last year - - time on the beach and climbing the bluff was wonderful, but the best part was seeing the students looking for and finding unusual flowers along the way.

"Kids are beautiful when they discover new things," she said.

For the past four years, she has been employed as dispatcher for the Island County Sheriff's Department. A reserve deputy for three years, she served for two years as secretary/treasurer of Island County Deputy Sheriff's Guild.

And in her spare time? She bakes and sews and digs in her garden. She used to be a member of Quilters on the Rock, but she works Monday evenings now, so she quilts on her own or with a friend. Jenna is learning to quilt and likes to work with her mother in her flower garden.

Jerilee taught basket weaving when her family lived in California and taught her oldest son the art before they moved to Coupeville. Her baskets were entered in the Coupeville Arts Festival for a couple years, "but that had to stop to give more time to my kids."

Jerilee carries her love of life into her relationship with her youngsters. They walk, read, go to the library and bicycle together, if there isn't a flat tire stopping them. They share a dog and several cats and she's able to be home for them after school.

"That's when they're ready to explode with things to tell about their day," Jerilee said.

There are no birthday parties in their house. They prefer to go to Bears in Oak Harbor, have some ice cream and go roller skating with friends.

And what about the clothes her kids wear? Well, both of her boys skateboard, so they wear the loose clothes, and that's okay, as long as they are clean, have no holes, and are hemmed above the shoe so there's no danger of catching in the rollers.

They do have to "look nice for special occasions and for church," which the family attends regularly. After that, as long as their grades are good and they stay out of trouble, she doesn't sweat the small things.

Jerilee believes parents should guide, not force kids. And instead of coming down on her kids, she chooses to ground them or take things away when there is a need for consequences.

The Gudmunsons will soon leave for Maryland. Just another move for a service family, some may think. But to those who know them, it's sad. A family working hard to make it in the world is wonderful to see.

I'm glad I got to know them a little bit, and that grandson Randy is counted among their friends. Maybe we are a little wiser for knowing the Gudmunsons and like Jerilee says, "it's hard to let go, but I'm learning."

Yes, we just keep on learning.

***

By the time this column goes to press, Gordie and I will be back from Bandon, Oregon where we celebrated our 16th anniversary.

Since May, we've been in more airports, gas stations and motels than I like to count.

We've been to births, graduations, weddings, anniversaries and reunions - - family and high school. Much as I enjoy seeing loved ones, I'm always glad to be home.

Except for two more trips in 1996, I plan to stay put for long time.

***

Cora's Advice: 'Imbibe a bit and have fun'

September 27, 1996

The Greenbank Bridge Studio was packed with players eager to start the game. But first there were six birthdays to be acknowledged.

Although each one was important, the star of the day was clearly Cora Bishop, 94 years young.

Cora was so excited she couldn't decide if she wanted to be interviewed or enjoy the best wishes from her friends.

We opted for a phone call later.

She talked about her apartment being "so full of flowers" and accepted compliments on the jacket she had made to wear on her birthday.

Illness had kept her away from the Bridge Club since January, so after they sang the birthday song and the candles were blown out, she was ready to play cards.

And play she did. Cora and her partner Pete Bender took first place. No, no one just let her win. Bridge players are highly competitive and no winner is "just lucky." It takes a lot of concentration and talent.

An avid bridge player for years, Cora was named the highest ranking Life Master in 1962. It was a great honor in the days when opportunities to compete were rare. Now, people compete every day and, she says, "all the young kids have passed me up."

After the bridge party, Cora went on to celebrate for another week. Her son came from Alabama for her big day and took her to Victoria, British Columbia to visit her sister. She has been there many times, mostly to "show off" to her guests from Virginia, but this trip was just for the fun of it, just to celebrate.

Cora is still on a high from all the excitement and publicity.

"I've never been that popular before," she quipped, "I might just have to be 94 again!"

Her advice for a good life?

"Imbibe a bit and have fun!"

***

Look forward to buying beautiful flower displays from Coupeville Garden Club every year at HarvestFest?

Don't worry. This year, the club's booth will be at the High School at the Uniquely Whidbey Trade Fair October 12 and 13.

***

For a couple who's "been behind schedule since May," the Bronsons do a lot of extras at their B&B, The Compass Rose.

Last week, they were called to house a bus traveler from the Bremerton Senior Center who had been ill and was ready to be released from Whidbey General Hospital.

Jan and Marshall said "yes" and picked up the lady and her husband, and provided gallons of fluids to the recovering patient throughout the night. Next morning she was fine and the Bronsons drove the couple to the Clinton ferry.

This isn't the first time they've had interesting activity at The Compass Rose but it always seems to come when all of the island accommodations are full. A couple Christmases ago, high winds stopped the ferry and a caller couldn't get home. She had no place to stay. Well, it was Christmas, so the Bronsons provided a cot for the woman in Marshall's study.

The woman's thank you note said "it was the best Christmas ever," which still worries Jan and Marshall.

The cot went up again for a guest who had ferried from Victoria to Port Angeles and biked to Port Townsend. No rooms were available in Port Townsend, but the traveler was told she could surely find a place on Whidbey. She did, in Marshall's study.

Right after they bought The Compass Rose, the Bronsons were called to pick up and house a couple at Whidbey General who had been in a boating accident. The Bronsons remembered being in a similar accident, and said "yes." The man's nose was broken and his eyes were black. His wife had fallen into the water.

Jan and Marshall cared for the couple overnight and went with them to take their boat back to Lake Washington. That couple has returned many times to stay at The Compass Rose.

The Bronsons are almost sure that other B&B owners have the same kinds of experiences, or just maybe there is a magnet somewhere on their property that draws people to them.

Maybe there are two magnets.

***

To donate to the Concerts on the Cove October 5 pre-owned treasure sale, call 678-1917 or 678-4684.

Night on patrol with sheriff's deputy an eye-opener

October 4, 1996

It was "time to belly up to the bar." I heard that phrase a thousand times growing up, and the meaning was clear. You said you would do it. Now do it!

Last week, I did.

A volunteer for the Island County Sheriff's Citizen Patrol, it was my time to complete another part of the training. A four hour ride-along with a deputy. I was picked up at exactly 5:20 p.m. and the minute we left our driveway, I had a greater respect for our deputies.

We were really 'out there'. Imagine. We were in a marked car, patrolling from Deception Pass to Houston Road. Alone. At any moment we could be called to stop a street fight no matter what kinds of weapons were being used, or to an armed robbery, or a domestic violence scene. Knowing the nearest backup was on the south end of the island, probably handling an assault, or a burglary, my heart was in my throat.

We responded to citizen requests, cruised the highway, drove into and around dark housing developments and resolved a juvenile problem at the request of Coupeville Marshal Lenny Marlborough.

At 9:05, I was grateful that I could go home and that it had been "one of the quietest nights in a long time." Then, the Navy called. They were detaining six youths who were intoxicated from alcohol and/or marijuana use on government property.

That the sheriff's department was called to the scene was a hoot for the kids. They said they weren't "doing anything wrong."

One had just been released from parole, and they all knew what would happen if they were arrested. They'd be told "no, no" and be released.

And they laughed about it.

Some of them had been picked up so many times the deputy knew their names and addresses. I was so impressed with his calmness and ability. Minutes after we arrived, the boys had wiped the sneers off their faces, the shouting stopped, and they had cleaned up their vocabulary to the point of apologizing if they even started to use foul language.

There is something very wrong with a system that believes juveniles who break the law repeatedly are "just going through a phase." These kids, so wise to the system, could be destined for much bigger and much worse things.

We must get our heads out of the sand for their sake.

The Sheriff's Citizen Patrol is made up of certified volunteers serving as extra eyes and ears for an extremely short staffed Island County Sheriff's Department.

While on patrol, volunteers report to the sheriff's office any unusual circumstances or criminal activity.

All volunteers must attend classes taught by the best in the field of law, communications, investigations, evidence and patrol procedures and complete training for CPR, first aid and safe driving.

Besides the ride-along, we are required to spend a specified amount of time observing the communications center and the county jail. Our background is thoroughly checked.

The citizens' patrol is part of Sheriff Owen Burt's community policing program making our county a safer place to live.

To become involved in the November classes, call Jim Nutt at 678-4422.

***

If you think being the mayor of Coupeville is a cushy job, follow Nancy Conard around for a day. When we were there, she had completed her normal work day at the school district, arrived at Town Hall after 3 p.m. and expected to be there several more hours.

***

Coupeville Arts Center's Judy Lynn, Emily Ramsey and Stella Canfield were walking on air Wednesday after being filmed for TV with their donated Rolls Royce.

***

County Deli has been a great place to eat for a long time. It's even better now that Dave Hamilton is employed there. Dave is also a construction worker and until recently, a loyal care-giver to Rob Workman.

***

Welcome Donna and Gus Barrett!

Married more than 40 years, the Barretts lived in Yakima before moving to Tacoma 10 years ago. After visiting their cosmetologist daughter Connie on Whidbey, they decided they "had" to live here. Gus is retired from Washington State National Guard, loves boating and fishing. Donna is a gifted knitter. They have five children and 20 grandchildren.

We're glad you're here.

***

Happy Birthday to Valerie Fuller-Howe and Jackie Riecks!

Meet Coupeville's year-round Santa

October 11, 1996

Santa Claus has an awesome beard, wears a red suit, arrives in a sleigh loaded with gifts for nice little boys and girls and comes once a year. Right?

Not on Whidbey Island. We have a Santa who gives away toys any day of the week on the streets of Coupeville or Oak Harbor.

His name is Max Hively.

Max has the beard and a twinkle in his eye. His sleigh is loaded with toys too. His "sleigh," though, is his motorized wheelchair or, if he's off on a special mission, his red jeep.

He visits hospitals, rides buses, sits in stores - - Ennen's is his favorite. He says he's not picky about who he gives his toys to. "A child is a child," he says, and all deserve a new toy every now and then.

Born in Etna Green, Indiana 73 years ago, Max lived in Tucson, Arizona for a while. He owned a boat and sailed to Whidbey a time or two. The last time, he had some "boat problems" that were too expensive to repair and too dangerous to sail in his physical condition.

So he stayed on Whidbey Island.

"At that point," he said, "I was just a Hoosier hot shot with a burned out battery."

One day, he gave a child a stuffed animal. The child was so excited Max decided to do it again. He started shopping garage sales for stuffed toys that were in "pretty good shape" and bought them when the price was right.

Max repaired the toys, and had them all cleaned. He built a rack and attached it to the back of his wheelchair, stuffed the rack with his toys and started down the street to share his bounty.

Every child he saw was offered the choice of any toy they wanted.

Playing Santa made Max feel so good that he's been doing it ever since.

Actually, the kids can choose any toy they want except one - - his "boss," Emmett Kelly. The puppet is the sad-faced clown he remembers seeing at a circus. Kelly drove his smoking Volkswagen into the ring, jumped out and opened the hood to check the motor.

But there was no motor.

Then, Max said, "a dozen huge clowns tumbled out of that tiny car." It still tickles him to think about it. Emmett rides atop of the rack, and there he stays.

Max has the red suit and around Christmas time, he distributes candy at stores and listens to the wishes of children. He does the Santa bit at churches, hospitals and by special request, at private homes.

He has a special place in his heart for children with Down's Syndrome. Last year, he appeared five times in a row, and it wore him out.

He's rested up now, and ready to go.

Max says he enjoys youngsters 2 - 6 years old.

"After six," he said with a chuckle, "it's pure graft."

He gets pretty upset with the older kids who tell the little ones there is no Santa: "It takes the joy out of the season."

Max tries to keep Santa visible. "Just try to tell a 4-year-old who has seen Santa that he doesn't exist," he said." It won't work."

He says benefits of his job are great. Once, after giving a toy to a little girl with ringlets, he said, "she grabbed my neck and gave me a big hug. Then she stood back and looked at me and said, 'You know what? I love you!' "

Yes, being Santa costs him money and time. But, Max says, "things like that make it worth every thing I have in it."

Max is forever replenishing his toy supply.

Sometimes he finds garage sale prices are more than he can pay, but when he tells the seller how he gives them away, the price is often reduced or they just give him the toys.

You can help Max too. If you have a stash of reasonably good toys your children are tired of, call him at 678-7404.

***

Dick and Betty Eisenbrey are proud grandparents of Isaac James Eisenbrey born August 14, 1996. Isaac joins his 5-year-old brother John. The Eisenbreys also have a great-grandson, Alexander, 6.

Congratulations!

***

Cat upset about missing dinner at Rosi's

October 18, 1996

Under the watchful eye of Tangueray the calico cat, Langley attorney Ken O'Mhaun talked to me on the phone Monday evening about his "big win" Sunday at the Uniquely Whidbey Trade Fair.

Ken may have won a night on the town, but Tangueray was still in charge. Ken said she was on the back of the couch *eyeing* him while we talked.

On Sunday, Ken signed up for a drawing at the Central Whidbey Chamber of Commerce booth. He won dinner for two at Rosi's Garden, and tickets to the David Howell Benefit Concert November 2, donated by Concerts on the Cove.

Ken's daughter, Heather, a postgraduate student in epidemiology, will be his date. He was thrilled with both prizes. They love Rosi's and have eaten there dozens of times.

And, Ken said, "I've heard so much about David Howell's voice, I'm glad I'll finally get to hear him sing."

Raised in Spokane, Ken O'Mhaun went away to law school, then returned to Washington to finish his schooling. In Olympia, he served three years as attorney for the State Supreme Court, three years on the House Judiciary Committee and had a private practice there.

In 1984, Ken decided he needed a place to rest. His friends, several long time residents of Whidbey Island - - some born here - - told him that Whidbey is the place to be. He came to the island and now considers himself a *native newcomer*.

"I've discovered more of who I am since I came to Whidbey," he said. For fun, he loves hiking in the high North Cascades.

He continues his practice and enjoys being a civil lawyer, likes some aspects of tax law, but he doesn't care for criminal law. Active in the community, he served as commissioner for the Port of South Whidbey and truly enjoyed working with the people.

One of the original planners of the Uniquely Whidbey Trade Fair, Ken was just an observer this time.

"It was strange to see something I helped get started going off on it's own," he said. He saw people who have been involved since the beginning and was happy to see that well over half were new local businesses.

He's hopeful that it's a sign of good things to come.

Congratulations on your win, Ken.

Enjoy!

***

Not to forget that cat. Tangueray is 10, and has been in charge for many years. She was named by Heather, Ken's daughter, when she was small. She thought Tanguery was a "distinguished" name for a cat.

Ken interprets the name as meaning "the way she wants it, is the way it is."

Tangueray controls Tzar, Ken's German shepherd, N'Kai, his Irish wolf hound, Rudy the ferret and life in total in the O'Mhaun home.

Cats are like that.

***

Congratulations to those who planned and participated in the 1996 Uniquely Whidbey Trade Fair. We had to go both days to see it all.

Great job!

***

Heather and Michael Roman have left Coupeville.

Lt. Roman, an A-6 pilot, was transferred to San Diego "to learn a new airplane." He will attend flight school in Pensacola, Florida until the first of the new year.

"The only thing good about the move," Heather said, "is my family lives in Pensacola, and we'll spend Christmas with them."

The couple came to Whidbey Island in December 1993. Heather was hired as director for the Central Whidbey Chamber of Commerce in March 1994 and worked there until early this year, when she was employed by Bill Bradkin at Coupeville Travel.

An active member of Concerts on the Cove, she was a board member and served as secretary. Heather and Molly McPherson were a wonderful team on many COC publicity projects.

"It is so sad to leave," Heather said. "I love walking down the streets in Coupeville and knowing everyone."

"I will be back to say *hello*," she promised.

We hope so, Heather.

***

Classmates get tours 'A' and 'B'

October 25, 1996

Mary Jo Isenmann answers her phone "Blarney Stone Retreat" and laughs. "It's an honest name, in honor of my Irish heritage," she says. Given her maiden name, Dooher, I had to agree.

When I called, Mary Jo had just finished a long nap after a teary good-bye to four guests from Oregon. This was their fourth reunion since 1953.

In 1990, Mary Jo retired after teaching for 30 years, and she had been ill. With time on her hands, she decided to reunite her classmates. "Sometimes it takes someone to be seriously ill before we recognize we need to get going," Mary Jo said, "to renew old friendships, to smell the roses."

Of the 11 classmates she found, eight came to that reunion. This time there were five, Janet, Louise, Betty Jean (BJ) and her dearest friend, Bruna. A sixth classmate, Pat, couldn't come.

They all started first grade at the same time at St. Mary's of the Valley Academy in Beaverton, Oregon and graduated from high school together in 1953.

"This reunion was the best," Mary Jo said.

They were on the run sightseeing for days, and spent their evenings enjoying movies, sharing photos and stories. Bruna showed them her memory books, something Mary Jo is now interested in doing, and they talked about the families - - all 24 children and 42 grandchildren.

There was little time to sleep.

Mary Jo is in love with Whidbey Island and is well prepared to share the island's beauty. Her guests are usually treated to Tour A or Tour B. She took her friends on both A and B.

Tour A goes north. Two of her friends are Master Gardeners and were thrilled with Hummingbird Farm. They visited Oak Harbor, then headed for Deception Pass.

She said she was worried about the pass, the "wind was so wild." She told her friends, "I'll drive, you pray." It worked!

The wind calmed.

Tour B took them for walks on the beach, to Ebey's Landing, and to Fort Casey. The women took their time enjoying everything they did.

It was a perfect time together.

They had a lot to talk about.

***

Get Ready for a stampede. We are going to be overrun by visitors in search of paradise. I just had a sneak preview of the brochure potential visitors will be sent when they call for Island County information. The November/December issue of *Sunset* and *Northwest Travel* list the toll free number.

Funded by Island County 2 percent money and created by an Economic Development Council committee chaired by Coupeville Mayor Nancy Conard, the brochure is the best I've seen.

It is beautiful.

We, on Central Whidbey, can be proud of the part our neighbors played: Nancy Conard, an expert director, led the committee in the decision making process; John Hitt, Nancy's alternate when her mayor/school budget director duties called; Don Storer, experienced in marketing, put forth his best; and Rita Kuller, a master in layout and design, lent her talents to the project.

If you were invited to view "majestic, windswept beaches ruled by tall, craggy bluffs," would you go? I would.

***

Susan McDonald and her mom, Ethel Kauffman, flew away a couple weeks ago on a non-stop birthday trip. Susan is home, but Ethel is still on the East Coast having a ball.

"We left Seattle on Mom's 81st birthday and Continental Airlines treated her like a queen all the way," Susan said. "We celebrated two of mom's granddaughters' birthdays - - Sarah's 8th in Zainsville, Ohio and Carmelle's 5th in Philadelphia, and then we celebrated my youngest sister Lorie's big day in Oakland, New Jersey."

OK, Ethel, the party's over. Come home.

***

Put your money where your heart is! Call United Way of Island County and pledge your contribution to a specific organization or your favorite area of need - - children, youth, the aged, whatever. Call 675-1778.

***

Sorry kids, no snakes, dungeons or torture chamber at 101 NE 7th in Coupeville this year. Just treats and pumpkins. Alice Martin, of the noted Halloween house, is taking a year off to plan for 1997!

***

Clark's diligence has made life better for disabled

November 1, 1996

Today, Sheri and Charles Clark move into their new off-island home. They will be missed.

Sheri moved to Oak Harbor from upstate New York in 1985 and, in 1986, married Charles Clark, a navy man she'd known for 20 years. They moved to Coupeville in 1988 and Sheri has been "whipping around" our town ever since.

Confined to a wheelchair because of a birth defect, Sheri learned to walk when she was 15, but once on her feet, she found walking was "way too slow" and went back to the faster pace of her chair.

She says she's never been one to "stay put" and has been told she gives disabled people a bad name because she does too much.

"I'm not going to stop doing what I want to do just because I can't walk," she said.

Her first job in Coupeville was at the Gold Nugget Jewelry shop in Mariner's Court. Sheri learned to make jewelry, and when owner Nancy Simpson was away, tended the store. Allergic to gold, Sheri just wore gloves and "kept on going."

After the Gold Nugget closed, she tutored a blind student at the Skagit Valley College, and served as docent at Island County Museum where she worked in the gift shop and helped with set up of the *Brothers of Cedar* display.

She attended weaving classes at The Coupeville Weaving Shop (now Elkhorn Trading Co.). To get there, she navigated the steps on her own, and "did" the Coupeville overpass in her chair - - alone.

"There isn't a flat place on that whole overpass. It only goes up and down," she said. "I wouldn't advise anyone in a wheelchair to try it - - use the signal light to cross the highway - - it's safer."

As a member of the Central Chamber of Commerce, Sheri chaired the Greening of Coupeville Committee, and was the attendant at the Visitors Information Center when it was located in the Harbormaster's office on Front Street.

At the VIC, she worked Tuesday through Sunday for months until she decided she had to have time to do other things she enjoyed.

Sheri belonged to the Society for Creative Anachronism (SCA), and was an active member of the Friends of the Coupeville Library where she performed her last duty at the national award ceremony for Carol Dyer. Sheri was in charge of Carol's guest book and made sure everyone signed.

"No one got past me," she said, "not even Mary Margaret!"

Sheri has made life easier for a lot of people by being adamant about the American Disability Act requirements. When the sidewalks on Front Street were torn up for repairs and she saw that no access cuts were planned for the curb, Sheri took her copy of the American Disability Act to Town Hall.

Because of her determination, Coupeville now has curb cuts on Front Street. She was also at then-Mayor Bob Lappin's side to see that ADA requirements were followed when the new ramp at Coupeville Town Hall was installed.

At the request of Coupeville schools,the Museum, and Oak Harbor businesses, Sheri conducted accessibility surveys which resulted in changes in Oak Harbor shops and in the display areas of the Museum.

In 1988, then-Mayor Bette Coyne appointed Sheri to the Citizen Advisory Committee for Island Transit. She served on that Committee for eight years as president and vice president and points with pride to the Paratransit division.

"We were the first transit in the state to be fully legitimate with the ADA," she said, "I carry card No. 7 of the disabled transit riders, and there are 300 to 400 hundred card carriers after me."

"Coupeville is a great town," Sheri said, "but it's the people I will miss."

Sheri, Coupeville is a better place to live because of your efforts. We will miss you.

***

Tickets are still available for the David Howell Concert Nov. 2. Call 678-4684 or 678-4453.

***

Gordie Mueller's 70th birthday was made much more palatable by Gary at Toby's Tavern.

***

The EDC brochure created by an EDC committee chaired by board member Nancy Conard was accomplished by Chambers of Commerce representatives from Whidbey and Camano Islands.

***

Santa gets an earful at Irene's

November 8, 1996

The excitement of Jason and Jordie, our 6-year-old grandkids, reached a level 10 on Sunday as they "helped" greet guests at Grandpa's birthday party.

Then Dan and Dorothy Jones walked in. The silence was deafening.

You know the Jones. They are the couple who dress in red and hold court at the Museum during the *Greening of Coupeville.*

Dan is perfect for the role.

He has a full beard and needs little padding.

The Jones weren't dressed in red Sunday, but Jordie recognized him immediately. She grabbed her dad's hand and when Dan walked toward her, she tightened her grip. Dan bent down and asked if she knew who he was - - Jordie didn't hesitate a moment.

"You're Santa!" she exclaimed.

Her eyes grew even larger when Dorothy showed her a picture of "Mr. and Mrs. Claus" from last year's *Greening.*

When Dan and Dorothy moved off to mingle, Jordie and Jason watched their every move. How could Santa be here, in Grandpa's house, dressed like everyone else, laughing and talking?

The twins whispered and giggled together and then disappeared. We found them in the kitchen in a huddle with Dan placing an order for a special Nintendo and other wonderful things.

It was beautiful.

***

The bonds go deep at reunions of old service buddies. Some of the friendships have lasted for 50 years. And while remembering the "war days" may be the reason they meet, sharing current interests is prime.

Last fall, Ben and Estelle Moja entertained 20 of Ben's WW II buddies and their wives at their Coupeville home. They just attended the national convention in Hampton, VA. Ben was in the 641st Squadron of the 9th Air Force 409th Bombardment Group. He was drafted in 1943 when he was 18, flew 60-plus missions and was discharged a staff sergeant.

***

Vern Arnold, a first lieutenant, flew B-17's with the 384th Bombardment Group out of an air base near Grafton Underwood, a little village in England.

About 200 members of the 384th meet every two years in a city selected the year before. Vern did his best to lure them to Seattle for 1998, but lost out to Hershey, Pennsylania.

Three of Vern's 10-member crew attended the reunion in St. Louis, Missouri in October and the search is on for a fourth member.

The group shared memories, then Vern and Peggy enjoyed the sights. Peggy overcame her claustrophobia long enough to ride in the gondola to the top of the 630 foot Gateway Arch.

"The view of St. Louis and the Mississippi River is spectacular," Vern said. Peggy's not talking.

The Arnolds also took a little side trip to Iowa to visit the kindergarten class of Peter, their 51/2 year old grandson.

Thanks to great airline fares, Peter and his mom and dad will return the favor in January.

***

22-year-old Bill Clark was earning $18 a week and the "Learn to Fly" posters were everywhere urging him to join the Army Air Corps. They promised to buy his clothes, his room, his food.

Bill signed up.

He graduated with the Flying Class of 1941-B from Maxwell Field in Montgomery, Alabama in March. Pearl Harbor was bombed in December. Like many, he was trained in a hurry to fly B-17s.

Bill retired in 1962, a colonel.

Bill's reunion was in Boothbay Harbor, Maine. Before the gathering, the Clarks took a "trip down Memory Lane." They viewed the Holocaust Museum, the grotto at Emmitsburg, MD, a replica of Lourdes, and spent a night at West Point. They also attended their grandson's wedding in Lynchburg, VA, visited friends in Gettysburg and their daughter in Washington, DC.

***

Air Force Major Bud Dorr was stationed in Ramstein, Germany, 50 miles north of Heidelberg, when he and three of his buddies met the four women they would marry. The women were civilian teachers hired by the Department of Defense to teach the children from the base.

Their first reunion was four years ago and included two other teachers who, Bud says, "weren't lucky enough to marry military men."

In September, the four service couples met in Cape May, NJ to talk, walk, and plan a third reunion in Coupeville this August.

Heritage search an adventure in Ireland

November 15, 1996

Janet Enzmann is one of the spokes of the Coupeville community wheel. She's everywhere. Working.

She's active in the Coupeville Festival Association (CFA), the Island County Historical Society Museum, Coupeville Library, and the Whidbey Island Genealogical Searchers (W.I.G.S.).

The Enzmann's have lived in Coupeville less than six years, but is seems they've been here forever. Janet came from Massachusetts to work at Seattle's YWCA and George from Minnesota as a Boeing engineer.

They met in Seattle in the 1950s.

After a couple Boeing employment squeezes, the Enzmanns moved on to work for airlines along the west coast. When George retired, they moved from Fountain Valley, California to Coupeville.

The Coupeville Festival Association caught Janet's interest, and she volunteered. After her first Coupeville Arts & Crafts Festival, she learned other CFA members, Sal Rizzo and Craig and Mona Van Velsor, had also come from Fountain Valley, and Emily Ramsey from Huntington, just a bit beyond. It tickles Janet that she ended up working with people from "her other town."

Janet chairs the on-going book sale at the library, and she's at the Historical Society Museum at least one day each week as the library archivist. She also organizes and does the bus and walking tours and "trots up and down" the streets of Coupeville reporting historical information to visitors, and now and then, "hops on buses" to do the same.

Sometimes, she meets tour buses at the Clinton ferry and "talks" the people all the way to Deception Pass. The last group "did lunch" at Old Morris Farm, she said, adding, "need I say more. It was wonderful."

In September, busy Janet disappeared - - no where to be found in Coupeville. She was working on her real love, genealogy. She had already traced George's ancestors (he's full German) back to the 16th century, so she went to Ireland to study her Irish culture and to chase the trail of her great grandfather who came to the United States in 1863.

This was her second trip to Ireland, the first one was for fun with her daughter, but this time Janet went on an Elderhostel program.

The group spent the first week at the University of Limerick on the river Shannon attending lectures on genealogy and taking field trips all over southwestern Ireland. The second week, they stayed in a mansion 20 miles north of Dublin and studied Irish art, literature, music, and history.

Then Janet went off on her own. She rented a car and for three days traveled the back roads of a land about one-third the size of Washington.

"Driving on the left side of the road is easy," she said, "but it was hard to *stay* on the left side while making turns."

Roads are wide and busy in and around the large cities, but a few miles out, the state highways do become very narrow, "equivalent to Madrona Way." The roads have no shoulders, and are flanked with 3-6 foot high rock walls or bramble hedges.

"I drove for miles and didn't see anyone," she said, "but believe me, when I *did* meet a car, I shrank to my side of the road and thought thin."

Janet ambled about, lost her way and enjoyed the scenery.

"Ireland is mostly pasture, with black and white sheep grazing everywhere" Janet said, "the countryside looks like a patchwork quilt created in 101 shades of green. It is beautiful."

She had planned to sleep at various places, but after spending the first night in Keadue with Peter and Margaret McNiff at the O'Carolan B&B in County Roscommon, she stayed put. "They were so wonderful I made the O'Carolan my base." Janet said.

She loved the small villages where everyone knows everyone.

"It's like Whidbey Island," she said.

She bought gas by the pound, ate tons of potatoes, turnips and rutabagas, and was amazed to see livestock of all kinds strolling the streets, "even saw a beautiful peacock strutting around like he owned the town."

Cattle gave her some problems, she said, "but, whenever they wanted the road, I just gave it to them."

Janet's great grandfather?

She was thrilled to find the 1849 handwritten record of his certificate of Baptism in the town of Keadue.

Janet took 12 rolls of film, and I bet if you asked her, she'd show them to you and maybe tell you a little about her trip.

Maybe even about the Elderhostel fellow from Massachusetts who turned out to be her cousins' dentist!

***

Trip to town, as always, an adventure

November 22, 1996

Going into Coupeville is an adventure. A couple Thursdays ago, that fact was reaffirmed when I went in to see my doctor, get a hair cut, have lunch and run a couple errands.

First stop an 8:30 appointment at my doctor's where I learned "mature adults" can be too clean. As we "season," our bodies produce fewer natural oils, and daily showering or bathing causes flaking and itching.

Maddening itching. I know.

I had changed soaps in the shower and in the laundry, questioned my supplements, and scratched. The doctor made sense, "Just how dirty do you get sitting in front of your computer?"

He was right! Think about it!

***

Next stop: PS Hair, where Phyllis Cook and Patty Blouin were planning their part of the Youth Dynamics Progressive Dinner, being sure there was enough china, stemware and silver.

I wish I had remembered to buy tickets to the affair. I should have. Phyllis told me 65 people enjoyed wonderful food and filled the coffers at the YD dinner. Appetizers were served at the home of Susan and Sandy Roberts, salads at Jacquie and Ben Vincent's, the entree at Patty and Scott Blouin's, and Alice Martin and Mark Franzen served the dessert at their home. Proceeds from the dinner go into a maintenance budget, said Phyllis, the dinner chairwoman.

"We have rent to pay and want to provide things for the kids to do. Probably buy new chairs," she said, "Kids are hard on things like that."

Mike Unruh, Island County YD director, is the youth leader of the Coupeville YD at 105 South Main Street, where high school kids spend a lot of time having fun and making plans.

"There is no booster club, "Phyllis said, "but YD is great for the kids, and we feel an obligation to help with the financial needs."

YD supporters meet every month and plan for future events. What are they? First, from 1-5 p.m. Sundays during December, YD kids will wrap your Christmas gifts - - they supply everything.

Secondly, you can order a Christmas tree to your specifications at Windermere, the official YD Christmas tree outlet.

Keep the tree and the gift wrapping in mind, and plan to attend the 1997 Youth Dynamics Progressive Dinner.

***

Went across the street to the Tyee for lunch where the newly-elected Chamber President Bill Thrailkill and Vice President Sue Hallen were doing the final count for their '*Greetings*' theater party fund raiser.

Today, I know the theater/dessert party was a huge success. The 120 seats at Whidbey Playhouse were filled. The play was delightful, the conversation a joy, and the desserts, enjoyed by everyone, were delicious.

Money from the fund-raiser will cover Chamber operations until 1997 memberships are due.

***

At Windermere Real Estate/Center Isle, my next destination, Susan McDonald was still excited about the David Howell Concert presented by Concerts on the Cove. David, one of the founders of COC, came 'home' from McMinnville to donate his time and voice to help reduce the pavilion debt. He and soprano Nancy Emrick, accompanied by Oak Harbor's Sharon Ringer, gave a first class performance.

David was in fine form and the beautiful Nancy Emrick flitted and flirted across the stage putting opera in a whole new light.

Perfect.

***

Coupeville Pharmacy was my last stop before going home. Cruising the aisles was a birthday boy in high spirits who wanted to be let in on the secret of what made the pharmacy smell so good. He seemed content when Bill said it was just pure vanilla scent.

Maybe so!

***

One thing is still unknown from that Thursday.

Tyee customer Mark Franzen acknowledged that his 40th birthday party last year was kind of expected, but he was one lucky guy to have a big celebration again this year.

KC and Dorothea Jones were at the Tyee having lunch and heard the conversation. KC stood up "You hear that?" he asked Dorothea, "Two years in a row! I only get a big birthday party every 20 years!"

Dorothea may have to do something about that.

Go into Coupeville, it's a wonderful experience.

***

Cancer survivor finds joy helping in the classroom

November 29, 1996

Thanksgiving is the time for us to be grateful for people who are good, kind, and make a difference in our community.

Harry Moore is one of those people.

Harry was 75 years old in October, and for Harry we are grateful.

The second week of July, he learned he had cancer and two weeks later he had surgery. Today, he has recovered with no chemotherapy or any medication. Harry walks a mile a day, surfs the net, and volunteers with a "capital V." He is one lucky guy and he knows it.

A Whidbey Island resident since 1976, Harry worked for Whidbey Press for 11 years in the pressroom and darkroom. After he retired, he decided he didn't do well sitting around resting.

So, during the seven years his daughter Sandra, a Coupeville High School teacher, served as advisor for the year book, Harry shared his darkroom expertise with students working on the project. He also worked with Don Wodjenski on pictures for the Island County Historical Society Museum's *Sails, Steamships & Sea Captains.*

Harry is involved with Beach Watchers too. He was in the second graduation class of Beach Watchers in 1990 and continues to work in water quality control for NOAA. Harry's favorite job with Beach Watchers started in 1993. He is on staff in the Interpretive Center at the Admiralty Head Lighthouse at Fort Casey where he does guided tours of the Fort and Lighthouse.

But the loves of his life are the kids in Sharon Bardwell's multi-age classroom at Coupeville Elementary. Harry volunteers at least two days a week, spending 2-4 hours in a one on one encounter with students helping them improve their skills in reading and writing.

But he does even more.

Sharon teaches important goals to her students; honesty, respect for each other and kindness. Harry enforces those goals. And the kids love it.

A couple years ago, Harry tried the "lunch buddy" route at the school, but found it wasn't *meaty* enough, so he moved on to school field trips. He's done everything from sitting on the floor in a Japanese restaurant enjoying the cuisine to carrying a pumpkin from the pumpkin patch for a little girl who found her choice "way too heavy."

Harry is sure that if adults knew how much fun they could be having in the classroom, they'd be volunteering right beside him.

If you have some time to share with the leaders of tomorrow, call volunteer coordinator Peg Tennant 678-4551 at Coupeville Elementary.

***

Coupeville's Joe Bellacera is recovering from his July shoulder surgery and working hard to get in shape for the encore after the first of the year. He says he wishes he'd had both surgeries "a long time ago."

Good luck, Joe!!

***

Don Matheson is a great neighbor. His lawn is meticulously kept, his flowers bloom beautifully, his house is flawlessly painted and his wrought iron gate is neatly closed.

And he helps his fellow man.

Dick and Arnell Hall were working on their dishwasher, and Don was right there to help. Wouldn't take a dime - - so the Halls corrected Don's one fault: he forgets to buy bird feed. A huge bag arrived at Don's door, and he did the right thing, he filled those feeders. And the flocks of birds descended. "They just came out of nowhere," he said. "It's right out of an Alfred Hitchcock movie!"

It's true. I wouldn't go so far as to say there are billions as reported, but the number is impressive and a little eerie.

***

Did you know? Brad Otten, quarterback for the University of Southern California is the son of Sid Otten who coached football at Coupeville high school in the early 1970's!!

***

Max Hively, our year round Santa, is worried that you tried to call him when his phone was out of service. He is always replenishing his toy supply and right now, close to Christmas, it's even more important that he have a good inventory.

Max will repair the toys your kids are tired of and give them to any child he sees. Max isn't picky, a child is a child.

Call him at 678-7404.

***

'Painting's what I've wanted to do my whole life-time'

December 6, 1996

Even as a child working in the cotton fields in western Oklahoma, Beth McBrayer knew that one day, she would be an artist.

"In the old days, everything came wrapped in heavy brown paper tied with string," she said. "My mother saved the paper for me and I would draw pictures on it with my crayons."

It wasn't until she was married, the mother of seven and living in California that she started using paints. When Beth injured her left shoulder, her doctor told her to paint for therapeutic purposes.

Finally, she *had* to do what she always wanted to do!

In 1981, Beth came to Whidbey Island and found the quiet of the island the perfect place to paint. She taught classes at Cam-Bey Apartments and to the developmentally disabled at the now defunct Tenex Industries. The job at Tenex was most rewarding. All of the students enjoyed the classes, but she was thrilled with one young man who wouldn't join in any activities, "Except, the minute I brought out the paints, he was first in line."

"The fact that I looked like his grandmother may have helped," she laughed, "but he loved to paint and it was awesome to see him come alive."

Beth managed Country Cottage Gifts for me in 1988 and 1989, and I was there when she sold her first large canvas, *Grandma's Attic*. A doctor from Snoqualmie walked in the shop, took the painting off the wall and paid the price. He also wanted to buy the copyright, but Beth said "No!"

She still sells postcards from that painting.

Grandma's Attic tells a story as all of Beth's paintings do. When she was a small child, her parents sold their home and stored some of their belongings in Grandma Martha Jane Carter - - of Carter's Pills - - Benton's attic. At age 16, Beth returned to visit and spent time in the attic enjoying her doll, her baby buggy, digging in old trunks, and in secret, her grandmother's love letters which were all bound in pink ribbon. All of the wonderful things she saw that day in the attic are in Beth's painting.

Family history is important to Beth. In her *Cottonfields* painting, her family is working in the fields, and across the road, children are playing in a school yard. Beth still feels the pain of the sharp points of the cotton bolls, and remembers wanting so much to go to school.

Wagon Yard, a painting of a "kind of motel" where the family stayed in Coalgate, Oklahoma, shows horse-drawn carriages and the many circus advertisements that covered the structure. She had never seen a circus and was enchanted with the pictures.

Beth has dozens of paintings - - each with amazing detail and each with a fascinating story.

But she doesn't paint much anymore. She was injured in a fall at a fast food restaurant in Oak Harbor in 1989, and she can only raise her right arm for short periods. So, with her left hand she brings the paper to the brush in her right hand and only uses water colors, a lighter medium.

"Painting is what I've wanted to do my whole lifetime," she says, "and at 79, I can stand that much pain."

Keep painting, Beth, and record those stories!!

***

Palmer Kauffman embraced the wonderful age of 85 on November 24.

That's how he lives his life, whole-heartedly. In his youth, Palmer was a civil engineer in New Jersey where one of his jobs was the construction of the George Washington Bridge connecting New Jersey and New York.

He and Ethel have lived on Whidbey four years. You probably know him. Palmer frequently delivers *The Coupeville Examiner* to local outlets.

Or maybe you've seen him driving around town with Lady BeeBee the Cockapoo sitting beside him while Ethel relaxes in the back seat enjoying the view.

Happy Birthday, Palmer, and many more.

***

Marshall Bronson celebrated his birthday last Tuesday. Marshall serves on the Coupeville Town Council, owns half of The Compass Rose B&B, is active in the Central Whidbey Chamber of Commerce and is in demand as speaker at most events in Coupeville.

***

Happy Birthday, Marshall! Happy Birthday, Gary!

Town Christmas parade filled with holiday cheer

December 13, 1996

Every person who braved the wind and rain to be in *The Greening of Coupeville* parade Saturday deserves a gold medal.

Mr. & Mrs.Claus waved enthusiastically, and we enjoyed the Marine reserve's "Hummer" for Toys for Tots. Our Town Staff held their own with snowman Nancy Conard (she could only see straight on in her costume), Larry Cort, as "The Grinch," Jean Hermanson as an elf, and Carole Wieldraayer and Pat Cozine, the gift boxes.

Somebody tell me who the wonderful "little gift boxes" were!

The best part was watching the little kids. Or was it watching the biggest kid of all, Peter Borden? Carolyn and Peter brought their grandchildren, Melissa, 5 1/2, and Joshua, 3, to see Santa. With every toot of the fire truck bringing Santa closer, Peter talked faster. And when Santa came into view, it was Peter who dashed for the street.

I wouldn't be surprised if Joshua got his wish..he agreed to sit on Santa's lap at the museum if his grandfather did too. Should have checked that out! Val Arnold says that Peter's excitement is nothing new. In the pre-Joshua days, Peter, with Melissa in tow, was first on the curb at the Memorial Day Parade.

The Bordens missed a couple years of their grandchildren's growing years while they lived in Georgia. Now that son Joshua and his wife Jan have returned to Bremerton, the Bordens are thrilled.

Carolyn and Peter have already had an exciting season. Carolyn's Mom came from California for Sarah Borden and Randy Harris's wedding in November. Sarah, a 1993 Coupeville High School graduate, and Randy, a Portland native, are stationed in Oak Harbor. The Harris's expect to remain on Whidbey Island at least until Randy's discharge in 1998.

***

The Marine Reserve's Toys for Tots barrels are just waiting for your offering. You can donate a toy at Whidbey Island Bank, Prairie Center Family Grocer, the county courthouse, or at Lumbermen's.

***

Most of the people who make living on Whidbey Island extraordinary don't see anything special about what they do. Two men top my list of people who make Whidbey special. Neither gave us their name nor asked ours. Shortly after we moved here, we needed a refrigerator. We found one at a garage sale and then wondered how we'd get it home.

No problem. A pickup truck arrived, the refrigerator was loaded and *the man* handed the truck keys to Gordie! A few weeks later on a cold Sunday morning, we hit black ice north of Coupeville, spun around, ruined two tires, and landed in a field. The first vehicle to come along stopped and *the man* brought us all the way home.

***

Barbara Lewis is a quiet lady who roasts a great Cornish hen. When she knows a friend needs a break, she delivers her fare to the door with all the trimmings. A royal feast.

***

Children who attend St. Mary's religious education classes think Margaret Hay is special. She's in the kitchen at Harris Hall with snacks every Monday afternoon when they arrive. There's always another cookie or another glass of juice, Margaret sees to that.

***

Carol Lee Hershman sends notes to people. If you have a sorrow, you'll get a note. She shares your pain and makes life easier. Do something nice? You'll get a note. She praises and encourages good deeds. Sometimes she just sends nutty cartoons or a funny article to brighten the day.

Carol Lee makes things happen. When Central Whidbey Chamber of Commerce volunteers were scarce for the collection and delivery of *Greening Day* materials to merchants, Carol Lee rounded up trucks and people, then joined the troops at the tree farm to load those trucks.

***

Chief Joe Biller, Central Whidbey Fire and Rescue, is a very nice person every day of the week, but when you call 9-1-1, Joe shines. Once he and his crew appear at your door, you know everything will be OK. His people are well trained professionals. And thoughtful. As they attend to the smallest details, they ease the fear with soothing words.

***

How about those Shifty Sailors. Isn't it special to hear them belting out a song about ships going aground because of the mooing of a cow? And isn't it easier to heed their advice the next day when you see them all decked out in their business togs?

***

Then there's Juan Gonzalez. If I didn't know better, I'd swear we were the only people on his mail route. He makes us feel special.

***

That's what it's all about. People make you special, that makes them special and that's what makes living on Whidbey Island special.

Library CD leads local vet to B-17 bomb group

December 20, 1996

Looking for a long lost friend or family member for your Christmas list? Vern Arnold found the solution.

The Oak Harbor Library has a nation-wide telephone directory on compact disk. The phonedisc has three parts: Eastern USA, Western USA, and Businesses. Enter the name you are looking for, and bingo, you are given a list of all the 'same names' from all over the country.

If you know the state, the search can be limited to that area.

The phonedisc doesn't contain every directory in the United States, but you might be lucky. Happy Hunting!!

Vern used the phonedisc while searching for the members of his B-17 Bomb Group for their reunion in St. Louis. He found his radio operator living just an hour out of St. Louis and he was able to join the group.

***

Louise (Chris) Christensen, active in the Coupeville community for 20 years, is now living in Edmonds "just loafing and getting reacquainted with Seattle and my old friends."

Chris lived on Front Street and was the faithful, unofficial custodian of the flower boxes on the street. She was the first to decorate for *The Greening of Coupeville* and the bows on her fence always looked fuller than any of the others.

Chris was a member of the Central Whidbey Chamber of Commerce, Coupeville Festival Association, Economic Development Council, Concerts on the Cove, and the Visitor's Council.

No more.

"I did my stint," she said. "I've finally learned what total retirement is!" Enjoying her "Proxy Family," the family of her long time friend, Clara Stenbakken, Chris attends junior high soccer games, birthday parties and school band concerts with Clara's grandchildren and is having the time of her life. She said she's found a proxy family where ever she lived, because "we all need to be tied to someone close by."

"I miss running into all the friendly people in Coupeville and I certainly don't have the daily view on Front Street, but," she added, "Edmonds is on the water, has a ferry, and the people are wonderful."

Best wishes in your new home, Chris, you are missed in Coupeville.

***

Judy Thorslund is a trooper.

Cutting across their adjoining yards to see her friend Page Gilbert-Baenan, Judy slipped and broke her left ankle in three places.

Wise or not, Judy hasn't let her accident interfere with her scheduled meetings for *Readiness To Learn* nor the middle school's *Power to the 8th* Retreat at Casey Conference Center this week.

Slow down, Judy, and put your foot up!

***

After nearly five years as Planning Technician for the Town of Coupeville, Pat Cozine's job came to an end on Tuesday.

In her honor, Julee Lawson and John Baldridge, owners of The Whale And Gator closed the door, shoved back the tables, and served a fabulous buffet which included their specially named crawfish cakes Cozine.

Joining the party were friends from Front and Main Street, former and current mayors Will Jones and Nancy Conard and the Coupeville town staff.

Pat worked for Consulting Planners David Nemens, Rob Harbour and Larry Cort, her current supervisor, who made the farewell speech:

"Pat is a valuable person, not only to the town, but to the community at large. Deeply committed to Coupeville, she has made it a better place to live. Pat volunteers in many organizations and even though her employment with the town is ending, her involvement in the community will not. This is just one small closure in her life. I expect Pat to always be a part of Coupeville. We look forward to working with her again in other areas."

Pat was presented with a print of the Coupeville Arts Festival poster created for 1992, the year she started with Town Hall.

***

Carol Peralta's supply of 'Christmas in Coupeville' sweatshirts is getting low, but if you're lucky, you can still order one in your size - - or one for a Christmas gift.

The logo and snowman for the shirts came from *Coupeville Examiner* editor Kevin Graves, but Carol added the snowman and put it all together. Stephanie approved.

Call CP Prints.

***

Happy Birthday, Vern Arnold and many more!

Toddler turning heads with fish hat

December 27, 1996

Carrie Ann Walker is only 31/2 years old, but she turns heads everywhere she goes. That's because she wears a purple "fish hat." The hat has fins, its tail waives above her brown curls, and its huge eyes are smack on top of her head.

Last week bankers stopped banking and County Deli customers stopped eating when she and her 1-year-old brother Andy and mom Cindy came into view. Carrie accepts all the attention gracefully.

Andy? He couldn't care less.

***

Those Central Whidbey Fire & Rescue guys did it again!!

They came Wednesday evening on their fire truck decorated to the Nth degree with a cheery "Merry Christmas," biscuits for the dogs, and candy canes for kids of all ages. Santa and his helpers lit up Inverness Way and made a very sick little girl feel a whole lot better. We thank you!

***

Vern Olsen's voice wasn't as hearty as it usually is when I talked to him Friday at Whidbey General, but his laugh was the same. Vern had surgery Tuesday after a couple weeks of major discomfort. He was glad it was over, and expected to go home the next day since "everything came out OK."

***

While Vern was recovering, his Shifty Sailors went caroling in downtown Coupeville. Dinners waited while Lumbermen's employees at Captain's Galley, and Whidbey Stationer employees at Christopher's joined in and sang along.

Customers at Toby's Tavern cheered when they heard The Sailors Prayer which begs for a sharp beaked dove to save them from "them blokes who sell bad beer to sailors," but they were quiet as they listened to a series of carols including Silent Night.

After the Shifty ones left, there was soft talk by men on bar stools about home and remembered family traditions.

***

Son Rick Fuller has returned to the island after eight years in California. He finds Whidbey as peaceful and beautiful as it was when he left, but busier. He and Penny are hoping to find work right here on the island and never leave again. Welcome home!

***

***

Late Nite Central is having a New Year's Party for sixth through ninth graders 7:30 - 10:30 p.m. Dec. 28th in the Coupeville High School gym. There will be games, prizes and snacks. Parents are welcome. Director Christy Chapman, a Coupeville Police Department Reserve, and Hank Toucher are always there and often, an Island County Sheriff's Reserve Officer, members of the Honor Society, and a board member.

Great place to play games or just hang out!

***

Max, our year round Santa, thanks you for your contributions. He spent last Monday at Ennen's Foods handing out candy donated by the grocer and your toys. He says that pretty much took care of his supply and he's ready to start collecting again.

Max has chosen the most precious donor - - a 6-year-old girl who filled a bag with toys and brought them to him. "They're her toys," her mom said, "she wanted you to have them." Max had a Santa Bear ready for a special child, "she fit the description," he said. She was tickled pink.

***

The Countryside Inn, south of Coupeville, is a wonderland with icicle lights stretching from end to end. Well worth a trip down Highway 20.

But Louise Harvey isn't satisfied. She and Gene Christopherson, owners of Countryside Inn, are a little behind in putting up their decorations this year. Both of them had a bronchial virus, and then friends came from Hawaii and Colorado so they've been getting ready for Christmas at a "turtle's pace."

Louise said she put soup on the stove and worked on her handmade gifts, taking them with her as she and her guests moved from room to room visiting. The decorating won't be complete until the sleigh and reindeer lights are on, and she expected that to happen before the end of the day. *Then* they will be finished.

***

This Christmas Season has been the most beautiful ever in Coupeville. Congratulations to Mayor Nancy Conard and to each of you who helped make it an extraordinary time.

***

A belated Merry Christmas to all ! I Wish You Peace.

Teens hear harrowing tales of drug abuse

January 3, 1997

We've made our New Years resolutions. Some we'll keep, some we'll just kind of forget about.

And it's OK for some.

It's not OK for island teens Nicole, Kendra, or Seth (last names are withheld to protect their privacy). Their lives depend on keeping their daily resolution to stay away from drugs.

Coupeville Middle School students who attended the *Power to the 8th* retreat in December know why it's so important to them. Nicole and Kendra and Seth told about their drug abuse - - their struggle to sobriety.

And they told it straight.

While they shared their stories, not one of the student in the audience moved. They listened, and they asked questions. Not much older than the students they were talking to, Nicole and Kendra, both 16, and Seth 18, hope they were heard.

If one person hears their message and changes their life, it's worth it.

Each talked of the pain they caused themselves and their families, of being alone and scared and of trying to break the chains. They told how they had hated the cops for busting their friends.

And how they blamed everyone else for their problems.

Seth said when he was 6, he watched adults sniffing paint thinner to get high. He tried sniffing, and more. He's been in treatment twice, nothing helped. Today, he's doing his best.

What did it take?

Seth, on drugs, couldn't make Thanksgiving dinner. It was the first family gathering he had ever missed. More than that, he knew his new sister-in-law was nervous about hosting the dinner and that she wanted everything to be perfect.

He let her down and it woke him up.

Kendra said she drank the leavings from family party beer bottles for as long as she can remember. She tried pot in the fifth grade and by the time she was in the seventh grade, it was an all-the-time thing.

She doesn't remember eighth grade, ninth grade is a blur, and by the 10th, she and her friends were using opium, acid and alcohol. Her life style wasn't accepted by her family, but nobody said "Stop."She thinks that maybe, if one person had said "No!" to her drug use, she might have stopped.

Seven months ago, Kendra realized she couldn't stop using drugs and everything crashed in on her. She knew her little sister was looking to her for guidance and her boyfriend was threatening to break up with her.

Her friend's mom was having a birthday and Kendra grabbed the lifeline. As a birthday present, she and her friend promised to stay sober for a year.

Kendra says her sober life is "awesome."

She was afraid the kids wouldn't listen, wouldn't accept what she had to say. But they did. At the end of the day, Kendra was walking on air and ready to go to work with young people in the fields of sexual behavior and drug abuse.

Nicole started stealing and using her parents' pot and alcohol when she was 12. She was "gone" on her drug trip for four years. Now, she stands tall, speaks straight and credits former Island County Sheriff Owen Burt with her success.

In an effort to stop increasing drug abuse on Whidbey Island, Burt brought an intervention specialist to the island. But how to reach the young abusers?

He interviewed young, recovering addicts and asked for ideas. Nicole told him her story and was one of three chosen to speak to the community. Burt was stunned by Nicole's story. She was stunned by his questions. He asked her what her goals were...where she thought she was headed.

She didn't know.

He made her think about her future. Made her make decisions.

She says Owen Burt saved her life.

Two threads run through the stories told by Seth, Kendra, and Nicole. First, now they know the "friends" who sold or gave them drugs - - the friends they used with - - were not their friends

Second, now free from drugs, they don't want to go back.

These young people already know what it takes some of us a lifetime to learn. They made a mistake. They are willing to put themselves on the line to help that one person who will hear.

Nicole, Kendra and Seth all deserve our respect, our help, and our congratulations.

***

Happy Birthday Sarah!

Mailman says he's now 'pain educated'

January 10, 1997

Juan Gonzales was at therapy and his wife Erin was busy making bread "the old fashioned way" when I called.

Juan is a Central Whidbey mail carrier. His route goes from Wanamaker Road to "the old Greenbank Cheese Factory" and back.

He's been on that route for almost 12 years. Juan knows the people on his route and he knows who's moved where.

He also works as community caretaker at the Bon Air development and, on Nov. 9, while clearing a lot, Juan slipped and hurt his back. "I heard something snap," he said, "and a couple days later, the pain started."

Standing, sitting, walking - - every move was painful.

He worked his route for two weeks before he had to give up. He was diagnosed with a herniated disk. The injury affected his sciatic nerve and caused burning pain to run down his leg to his ankle. Two months later, that pain has receded to his upper thigh.

The healing is slow...like taking baby steps. The first month, he stayed flat on his back. In December, he was able to alternate between sitting and lying down for short periods. With chiropractic care, massage therapy and therapy at Whidbey General Hospital, he has come a long way.

This is the first time Juan has ever been hurt. In fact, he's never had any problems. Never had an operation, never even stayed in a hospital.

He is glad he isn't where he was a month ago, "I have nothing to complain about," he said, "I've been 'pain educated', and now I have true empathy for people who hurt."

It's been a humbling experience in a lot of ways. Before his fall, if it had to be picked up, Juan picked it up. If it had to be done, Juan did it. Not anymore.

The worst part is the wounding of his Latino pride. "We're the men, we can take it. Right? We take care of the women. Now here I am, after 15 years of marriage, my wife has to put my socks on for me! That's humbling."

Juan, who says "this do nothing business is getting pretty old," expects to be back on his route in a few weeks. In the meantime, he has a lot of things going for him.

He has a wife who takes six loaves of whole wheat bread out of a hot oven every Monday morning.

He's spending a lot of time reading and playing games with his three children, Jarin, Valencia, and Amorita, and all the people he serves are anxious for him to recover and return to his mail route.

***

There were three immediate responses about congratulations extended to Kendra, Seth and Nicole in last week's column.

"Not to take anything away from the young people for cleaning up their act, but how about their parents and other family members who weathered the terrible storm?" and "How about the sleepless nights, the fear and the pain?"

We should have remembered those who stand by as their loved ones attempt to destroy their bodies and minds.

If you have experienced the horror or are experiencing it today, your agony is recognized.

Consider yourself hugged.

***

The recent storms caused a lot of damage but they also brought out the best in many people.

Puget Sound Energy and Light crews, working in raging winds and knee- deep water were quick to fix the no lights — no heat problems. And Good Samaritans were busy helping strangers and friends to dig out driveways and pick up groceries for those too timid to drive.

Gary Smart left his home and family Christmas night to rescue a young lady trying to catch the last ferry back to Seattle. Jenny Grant's security system locked her out of her running car and her extra keys were 50 miles away. With Smart's help though, she made the ferry.

And the grandson of a previous owner of Tyee Cafe, a navy man with two days off, took it upon himself to relieve the water pouring over the road and into the yards along Engle Road.

"Here he was," Elizabeth Hancock said, "on his days off, wallowing in the muck, unblocking the drains along the road."

"He was wonderful," Elizabeth said.

Wonderful people do live on Whidbey Island!

***

Happy Birthday, Jason & Jordie!

Take time to talk — and listen — to kids

January 17, 1997

Parenting.

That's a big word. And a big job. Dozens of books have been written on how to parent and how not to parent. Everyone has the answer — especially those who aren't parents.

This week I've heard five people who do have children speak about being an effective parent. They made sense. They talked about having weekly family meetings in a safe environment. Meetings that recognize the importance of each person. A time to validate needs...time to share pain...time to hear dreams.

It's hard to be a kid ...it's hard to be a parent.

We need to listen, we need to hear. We can't listen, nor can we hear, when the television is blaring. What if it were quiet.

What if we turned the television off. What if we turned it off one night every week? What if we read a book together or played Scrabble as a family. What if we talked. Do we remember how to talk? Do we remember how to listen?

What if we talked to kids in a positive manner? What if every single day we said "You are one great kid" and "I love you" and "You can do it!"

What if we were positive in our attitude? What if the punishment for every infraction were equal to the "crime." If a child comes home an hour past curfew, how about an hour of wood chopping?

Kids understand the need to give back what they take. Why restrict him from a TV show you didn't want him to watch in the first place to make up for that hour?

Do you say "How many times do I have to tell you to hang up your jacket?" Do they care how many times you've told them? They couldn't care less. How about "Your jacket must be moved...to the closet... or to the Goodwill." But, you have to mean it, and the child has to know there will be no replacement. You want your kids to have choices? Let them make the choice!!

We must also provide an environment for the development of our children's talents. Pay attention. Kids do things to get feed back - - whatever brings them strokes or warm fuzzys. Whatever their talent - - organization, creativity, or doodling, focus on what they do. Your child will develop those talents and branch out as his interests expand and those doodles, in whatever form, will ripen into a successful career.

Happy parenting! Give it your all.

***

At 8-weeks-old, with her smiling blue eyes, McKayla Jean Bailey held court at Tyee Cafe on Tuesday. McKayla's parents, Russell and Donna Engle Bailey, Jr. and her uncle Bob calmly ate their lunch as Mary Anne and McKayla carried on a spirited conversation with customers.

McKayla is an eighth generation Coupeville Bailey and at least a sixth generation Coupeville Engle. She was born Nov. 13, and her favorite hour of the day is 5 a.m., which is a couple hours earlier than her mom and dad prefer.

Both parents are graduates of Coupeville high school - - Rusty in 1987 and Donna in 1992 — and are employed at the Engle Farm.

***

What are the odds?

For three years, Don and Michelle Swerdfeger, owners of The County Deli, have purchased season tickets to the Paramount Theater in Seattle, and they always have the same seats.

At Christmas time, her Everett cousin, Jeanine, told Michelle she had tickets to a play. Michelle thought that was nice, but didn't ask when or where.

Then she and Don went to the *Master Class* performance. Who sat next to them with season tickets? Her cousin Jeanine.

The Paramount is one big theater.

What are the odds?

***

Oops...Went for lunch and asked for a table for two.

"She'll be here in a minute, and could we have the table by the window?" I asked. The table was a four seater, dirty, but empty.

"Sorry," she said, "this is our busy time, please sit here."

I settled into the two seater in the middle of the room and the two men directly behind me asked for the table by the window.

"Sure," she said, "just give me a minute to clear it."

***

Happy Birthday, Katie!

Elvis spotted in Coupeville dining room

January 25, 1997

Remembering this is 1997 is a tough task when you visit the home of Bill and Bernice Bainbridge.

Bernice works in the Island County Treasurer's office, Bill is a land surveyor and works at Lumbermen's, and they are serious, selective, collectors of nostalgia.

Bill collects old neon beer signs, Bernice collects Elvis memorabilia, and they've both collected records since high school.

When Bernice, Anacortes High School Class of 1966 married Bill, Coupeville High School Class of 1965, they combined their treasures and continued collecting things together. Twenty three years later, they own 25,000 records, a recreation room from the past, and a room full of Elvis memorabilia.

Bernice has created an Elvis Room that fans of the King would die for. A full-size, free-standing Elvis watched my every move as I viewed his signed scarves, pictures, albums, posters, statues, gold records, the clock, the phone, the lamp, dog tags, and ticket stubs to his concert at the Coliseum on April 29, 1973. Section 80, Row 4, Seat A.

Bernice has visited Graceland three times and may go again. She has seen Elvis collections touted on TV and in newspapers.

"My collection beats them all, " She said. "Am I a fanatic? If 'fan' is short for fanatic, I guess I am!"

Step into the dining room, and on the wall, a guitar inscribed with *Elvis* in neon glows above a 1952 vintage ROCK-OLA. "The juke box, a working tube type, isn't played very often," Bernice said. "The tubes hum and give me a migraine. It isn't practical anyway, the tubes are expensive and difficult to find."

Book cases display Elvis books and behind closed doors are boxes and boxes of old 45's all obviously cared for by an expert.

Go into the rec room and step back in time. Old neon beer signs line the walls, there's a pool table and popcorn machine, and an old penny scale that gives your weight and tells your fortune.

There is a wind-up RCA Victrola to play their 78's and a 1980 Rowe juke box for their 45's.

All the records Bill and Bernice have collected were recorded between 1949 and 1967. There are a few from the late 1960's, but they are not hard rock. Hard rock they don't like - - they collect only what they enjoy.

Bernice has catalogued all of the records in her computer and can access any year, title, or artist. Ask, and they will bring their record player, speakers, a few thousand 45's, and play your kind of music for you.

They've done weddings, class reunions, dinner parties, and a benefit at the Coupeville Recreation Hall.

"Someone would donate $1 to play a song, and someone else would pay $2 if we didn't play it. That was fun."

If you just want a tape of your favorites, they'll do that too. "We love the music, and taping gives us another chance to enjoy it."

The old license plates and some of the records displayed at DJ's diner in Coupeville are from the Bainbridge collection.

They use to donate duplicate records to thrift stores, but friends 'found' the records and brought them back. Once, they were presented with a box full of records — the same box they had donated to a Burlington thrift store the week before.

They've decided to hold their own garage sales. It's safer.

Bernice worries about old records people have in their basements or attics.

"Neither place is good," she said. Records must be dust free and kept in a temperature controlled area. And don't stack them on top of each other. Sleeve them properly and stand them on end.

"Sometimes they can be cleaned, but they become worthless once they are bent."

Bernice and Bill upgrade their collection whenever they find a record that's in better condition than what they have. And even though they would have to build another room just to display the rest of Bernice's *Elvis* collection, they keep looking for more things from the 1950's.

Since they never sell anything, what if they find something else?

Bernice isn't worried, "Trust me," she said, "it's enjoyable — whatever happens."

***

Tendonitis leads to profitable venture

January 31, 1997

Tendonitis isn't something anyone wants, but the affliction changed Marcia Comer's life for the better.

Her typing days as a legal secretary over, Marcia went looking for something else to do, and she found it.

For years, Marcia and her friend bottled a variety of vinegars and gave them away as gifts. They decided to expand their product line and go into business. In 1993, Mutiny Bay Gourmet began in Mukilteo and two years later, the Comer's, Whidbey residents for 20 years, bought out the partnership and moved the business here.

The herbs, spices, and berries are all produced on the island. Packaged beautifully, each unit has a label with a window "so the customer can peer into the highest quality product they will find."

The label has a nautical flair and, since people like to take a bit of the island home with them, Whidbey Island is part of the logo.

Forty specialty shops in five Washington counties carry the products: five vinegars, five spice mixes, and three jams.

The business is still growing. "Ever since we started I've been told that the economy is slow," she laughed, "Good thing it's slow, or we would never be able to keep up."

Featured in *Seasons on Whidbey*, Mutiny Bay Gourmet will soon be highlighted in the *Taste of Home* magazine. Recipe sheets, free at the outlets, include the *Mutinous Mollusks*, a winner in last year's Captain Whidbey Inn Mussel Festival Contest.

Born in Everett, Marcia gives a lot of the credit for her success to her father, Marv Jacobsen. As a child, she spent time at his business, Jacobsen Brothers Boat Works in Arlington.

"The goal of Mutiny Bay Gourmet is to operate as my dad did in his business," Marcia said, " to work hard, always be honest, and to produce a quality product."

"My dad calls it the Norwegian mentality."

That Norwegian mentality seems to be working!

***

***

Any boy will tell you girls have more fun.

If girls do, it's because of people like Trish Sullivan and Teri Carey, leaders of Coupeville Girl Scout Troop No. 154. This is Trish's fourth year as leader and she says she has just as much fun as her Scout daughter.

"There are so many opportunities," Trish says "and no one is left out. Every girl from every income bracket is offered a variety of exciting ways to earn badges."

To help the Scouts earn their Jewelry Merit Badges, Frank Nold of Jewelry by Lee gave a special presentation at his shop. He told them about metals and stones and showed them his vast bead selection. Frank was impressed with the questions the Scouts asked him. "Their curiosity showed very mature forethought," he said.

Eleven girls attended the session, Sarah Sullivan, Melissa Carey, Tiffany Folkstead, Amanda Hertlein, Tracy Wait, Kim Bott, Bronwyn Russell, Brianna Phillips, Lena Messengale, Alicia Landry, and Ashley Tingstad.

"In Scouts," Trish said, "the girls are taught leadership skills and how to solve problems in their lives."

Last year, Troop 154 visited the Science Center, rode horses and learned about their care, (horse ownership not required) and went camping several times off island. "This year," says Trish, "we'd also like to pitch our tents at Camp Casey or on Ebey's Prairie."

The boys might be right, maybe girls do have more fun.

Your daughter, kindergarten through high school, can be a Girl Scout. Adults can enjoy Scouting too, leaders are always needed.

Call Shirley Jolly 678-4188.

***

Congratulations on your 51st Wedding Anniversary
Adolph and Dolores Meisch!

Real Estate broker: Island sells itself

February 7, 1997

"My gosh, there's no one here! What will I do!"

That's what Leona Aaker of Loganberry Hill Realty thought the first time she drove up the island in 1971.

Twenty six years, and thousands of happy clients later, Leona wouldn't do anything but be at 3084 S. Highway 525. She says she loves the Greenbank area and the people.

"The best thing about working in this area is that once the client moves in, they are your friends for life. Of all the clients I've had, there are probably four or five I wouldn't want to see again," Leona said. "It's not hard to sell property here. Once they're on the island, people know they've found where they want to be - - it's just a matter of finding where they'll live."

A real estate agent for over 35 years, Leona moved to Whidbey Island after a dinner conversation in Seattle with Tom Page, a family member. Tom invited her to join him as his partner in his Whidbey Island realty business. Two years later, Tom retired and Leona was on her own. By then, she knew she'd do just fine.

Besides her children, Kate and Cliff, and her realty office, Leona's world includes the buildings that house the Besta´ Round Pizza and a new shop where Browne, Youngberg & Nowak prepare taxes.

Congratulations to Leona and her Loganberry Hill Realty!

***

Ever since Peggy Yuska moved to Coupeville last fall, she has been raving to her parents in Indiana about our island. So the Yuska's came to see this place that sounded "too good to be true."

They found the area to be as wonderful as Peggy said it was and they made friends.

Leonard, Peggy's dad, and Palmer Kauffman, both retired engineers, found lots to talk about, had lunch together at Toby's Tavern, then Palmer took him on his *Coupeville Examiner* delivery route. What better way to show him the town!

Maybe you saw them, two friends in their 80's enjoying life to the hilt.

***

Tyee's Sue Hallen took a couple days off work for surgery, and was right back on the job. Her doctor might not approve of her time frame, but Sue said she's feeling great.

***

During our last big storm, John and Peggy Davis had company from Festus, Missouri, daughter Janet, her husband Paul, and Jonathan, their 15-year-old son.

The house was bustling, and as usual, when things get hectic, Heidi, their cat, disappeared.

Peggy said she wasn't worried, but a couple days later, they found her lying in the street. Family members gathered and with umbrellas in hand, they held an appropriate burial for the cat who had been a part of their lives for 8 years.

Then lo and behold, Heidi was back. She showed up on their doorstep hale and hardy.

The Siamese the Davis' had shed tears over and buried so carefully, belonged to someone else.

"I'm sorry for whoever the owners were, they should know what happened."

Heidi, it seems is living on borrowed time.

"Whenever she pulls one of her 'cat things', I tell her 'Look out Heidi, I buried you once, I'll do it again'," Peggy laughed.

***

Next time you pull into the Hancock Lake Overlook just north of Greenbank to view the sunset, to watch the fog lift to reveal the mountains or to gaze up to the stars, thank yourself and the people of our community.

If it weren't for the courage and action taken by so many to protect this most beautiful place on Whidbey Island, the Lake Hancock Overlook might have become a 30-plus parking lot for Island Transit!

You did it!

You came as ordinary residents and as representatives of organizations from all over the island. You wrote letters and met with the state Department of Transportation and Island Transit many times.

Dozens of you showed up in freezing weather for the park-in protest at the lookout last Saturday, or honked in support as you went by, and you came in droves to express your views at the meeting at the Greenbank Community Clubhouse last Friday.

In the end and $40 thousand dollars later, DOT officials said they had made a mistake.

They promised that in the future, they'll ask before they do.

Yes.

After the Facts offers students fun, variety

February 14, 1997

Coupeville Middle School students do have something to do!!

Wednesdays, after early dismissal, they can stay at school and drop in on eight classes not available during a regular school day.

Through *After-the-Facts*, individuals and organization representatives volunteer time to help students develop special interests and hobbies.

The list is impressive. Whidbey Island Genealogy Society, Oak Harbor School of Tae-Kwon-Do, Whidbey Island Radio Control Society, Audubon Society and the Coupeville Arts Center. A special grant from the Coupeville Festival Association funds the Arts program.

After-the-Facts is provided through the L.E.E.P. grant (Law Enforcement Education Partnership) and sponsored by the school, Central Whidbey Youth Coalition, the Island County Sheriff's Department and Coupeville Police Department.

Director Christie Brookman invites your comments, suggestions and any volunteer time you can give. Call Christie 678-9050.

Classes change week to week, so check the Community Calendar in *The Coupeville Examiner*.

***

Congratulations to the Coupeville seniors and teacher Barbara Ballard for an extraordinary production of *The Tempest*.

***

The Seattle Peace Chorus gave an outstanding presentation of "Mother of Us All" Sunday. The Chorus returns to Coupeville in May to join the Pozo Almonte Municipal Choir sponsored by Concerts on the Cove.

***

Even as you read this, there's a murder happening in Coupeville. Soroptimist International of Coupeville members are holding their "Fun Raiser" Mystery Dinner and somebody is going to get 'it'.

I'll let you know who!

***

Rita's Rainbow Thrift & Gift Shop, chock full of wonderful items from teapots to beautiful jewelry, celebrates its second anniversary today with chocolate candies for the customers.

"It's my way to say thank you," Rita Kuller said.

Rita says she became the owner of the shop via "two moments of reinvention." After majoring in fine arts, she painted and created beautiful things. Suddenly, that wasn't possible anymore.

So Rita reinvented herself.

She went into the printing business, rose to production manager in Wisconsin and continued in that field when she moved to San Francisco. Hired by a record label company in Los Angeles, she became involved in the entertainment world and represented celebrities. It was a great job, fun, interesting, but Rita had had it. She was ready to get out of LA — to do something else. She traveled around looking for "home."

She couldn't find it.

She remembered a young man at the record company who never stopped talking about the beautiful place he came from. A thousand times he described the sky, the mountains, the changing seasons, and always the people. It took her three months to track him down.

He told her to "Get on I-5 north and turn left at Mount Vernon."

Instead she arrived by ferry on a rainy winter morning.

"The minute I got off the ferry I knew I was home." She loved the island, but still, it took years to make the move. Realizing her resume of promoting celebrities wouldn't get her a job on Whidbey Island, Rita went into middle management in the investigative and legal professions.

She didn't forget the island. "I'd sneak up here in the middle of winter expecting the worst and see splendid gray skies."

"No matter when I came it was beautiful....except once....not bad for 10 years!"

In 1993, she joined her mom, Dulcy, who was settled in Coupeville and "happy as a clam," but Rita found no job in her field.

So Rita reinvented herself for the second time.

With no retail experience, she became a shopkeeper and Rita's Rainbow Thrift & Gift Shop and Coupeville became the loves of her life.

Rita believes "everybody must give something." She is a member of the Coupeville Festival Association, the Economic Development Council, environmental groups, and serves on the board of directors of Central Whidbey Chamber of Commerce and Concerts on the Cove.

In October, Rita's past caught up with her. Larry Sellars, who plays Cloud Dancing, the popular Native American on CBS TV's Dr. Quinn, Medicine Woman and Graciela Casillas, the internationally respected martial artist, hired her to represent them.

So Rita opened a second business, *RainShadow Public Relations*. The contracts came with strings. Rita told them she won't be flying around the country much nor will she be at ringside. Because Rita's Rainbow Thrift & Gift Shop and her community come first.

Didn't there used to be a house there?

February 21, 1997

I find people and places by following landmarks, so when I see buildings raised and movers at the ready, I get nervous.

Maybe you do too. If you've come back after 20 years, you might think your memory is bad.

It's not. The buildings aren't where they used to be.

Start with Gerri and Tom Strang's *Woodcraft Of A Simpler Time* on Coveland. It moved twice, from Front Street to where the condos stand near the wharf, and later to its present site. Bill Bradkin's *Coupeville Travel* was moved to Coveland from the museum site on Alexander.

The *Coupe-Gillespie House*, part of *The Inn at Penn Cove*, was built where the courthouse stands for Captain Coupe's daughter Keturah and her husband James. The house was moved a couple blocks east before being moved to its present site by then owners Barbara and Jim Cinney.

Beautiful as it is, our Museum's records preface the style description with Vernacular and some long time residents say it's Coupeville's oldest mobile home.

The *John and Jane Kineth House*, the other half of "The Inn," hasn't moved at all, but is listed in the *Daughters' of Painted Ladies* by Elizibeth Pomada and Michael Larsen.

Built in 1887 as a retirement home, it was known as the "Blue Glass House" because of the Evening in Paris cologne bottles in the windows. When owners Judy and Claude Harvey saw Pomada's book, they wanted a Painted Lady of their own and chose as their color scheme - - rose, blue, and cream.

Unacceptable.

"At first, as towns people pulled out from the post office across the street, (now the County Deli) they shouted complaints," later, the Harvey's said, "You'd think it was their idea to do it this way. People think we did lots of restoration of brackets and gingerbread, we didn't. It was all here, but you couldn't see it because it was all white."

This classy confection is also on the National Historic Register.

There have been other changes to the Kineth House, current owner Mitchell Howard says, "In the book, of course, the Cinney sun porch isn't there, and there was a triangular flower garden where the sign is."

The Hawthorn tree, which worries Mitchell, still stands.

Neal Amtmann's *Hole in the Wall* has wandered all over Front Street serving as an abstract office and a meat market before coming to rest to serve the best ice cream cones in town.

The *Lee James House* on Broadway and Terry, just moved down the road and *the brown shingled house* moved back when the highway moved near by.

The *First Methodist Manse* from the Prairie Center area was purchased by the Coupeville school district, rented to teachers, then moved to Ninth and Otis. The two *rentals* near Sixth Street park were barrack homes at Fort Casey.

Captain Thomas Coupe's house has been moved back from the bluff twice due to erosion. I'm told the road was in front of the house on the water side. Because of the moves, the mighty black walnut tree that stood in the back yard, now graces the front yard.

The house that sat where Mariner's Court is now, resides at Ninth & Gould, and the *pointy topped* houses on Haller were moved to town from the prairie.

When you visit *town hall*, you are walking into a building that was once on Wanamaker Road and served as the caretakers residence at Fort Casey pumping station. It was moved to town when the town bought the Fort Casey water system.

Fairhaven, behind the museum, was built in 1852 in Coveland by Jacob Smith, purchased by Swift, and in 1928, disassembled by Swift's youngest son and moved log by log across Penn Cove and reassembled. Hattie Swift Race was born in that house across the water in Coveland and died in it in Coupeville.

Just the tip of the iceberg of Coupeville houses that have been moved from here to there - - and how they got there.

It worries me. I hope they don't decide to move the Anchorage Inn or the Methodist church.

I'll never get where I'm going!

***

Ethylee Maylor may be tiny, but she's mighty

February 28, 1997

She's no bigger than a minute, so when I met Ethylee Maylor, it was hard to imagine that she could have moved houses 55 years ago. After talking to her, I'm a believer!

Married to Ted Maylor for 48 years, they worked together on their farm on Maylor's Point until the property was requisitioned by the Navy in 1942. The Maylor's bought property in Scenic Heights, and hired a man from Burlington to move their buildings to the new site.

"There were times when the fellow was in pretty bad condition," Ethylee said, "so I drove the moving truck !"

"Besides our buildings," she said, "we moved the Mitchell's to Crescent Harbor and another family to Burlington."

A 1928 Coupeville graduate, Ethylee Anderson went to business school in Everett where she was top student in her class of 12. She accepted a job with 'Ma Bell' in Petersburg, Alaska in the days when sweeping the floor, making coffee, and doing the dishes were part of the job description.

Ethylee has used her switchboard experience in other jobs, but she likes people and prefers seeing them face to face. After leaving Alaska, she worked in Everett, at her aunt's dry cleaning business and grocery store where, she says, "if I'd been smart, I would have opened an ice cream parlor there, but I didn't."

Ethylee finished two years of nurses training at Everett General in the days when "a nurse was just a nurse."

She beams when she tells that her granddaughter is a nurse in cardiology: "If grandma did it, I can do it."

Ethylee found both the business world and nursing too confining. "I've always had itchy feet - - I want to go places and do things."

And she does. Her son has the family farm at Scenic Heights, but she keeps her hand in, and now's the time to plant potatoes.

To this North Dakota farm girl, the word potato brings memories of miles and miles and tons and tons. Ethylee says not to worry, she may be a Swede, but she eats more potatoes than her Irish husband ever did!

During the 1970's, she was groundskeeper at the Olympic Bank in Oak Harbor and when that wasn't enough for her, she took landscaping classes at Skagit Valley College. She was the only female in the class, she soon found out people weren't too exited about hiring a lady landscaper.

Today, Ethylee does a home on West Beach Road, works two days a week in the yard at Fairhaven, then volunteers at the museum two more days a week. One of those two days, she tends the museum grounds, but never on Sunday.

"Sundays, I wear a dress and it wouldn't be proper," she said.

This lady is one ball of fire. There's a sparkle in her eyes and her energy and ease of movement would challenge a woman half her age. She says she "lives for tomorrow" and has her program for the day all set.

Ethylee didn't say so, but I knew I was interrupting her program. During my phone call Friday, she was suddenly talking about all the work she had to do in her yard.

On Sunday, she very neatly walked me out the museum door.

***

Visited grandchildren KayLynne and Emily (and their folks, too) in California last week. Two year old KayLynne loves to play ball. Kicked like a pro with her left foot, then marched across the lawn to make sure we kicked it back the right way.

I found if I squinted, I could see her daddy at that age marching across the yard in Minnesota with the same gait and determination. Amazing.

Have you been to Long Beach in February? Bougainvillea, camellia and impatiens are blooming, and there's a tree with tiny white flowers that smells heavenly. We sat in the back yard in the evening and the breeze carried the aroma to us.

It was incredible.

***

Dana Blouin, Coupeville resident for 35 years, wants to know what's going to happen to the Hancock Lake view when the hundreds of trees planted below the highway reach full height?

***

Happy birthday, Wylie Vracin!

Co-op Preschool to hold its first fund-raiser Saturday

March 7, 1997

The classrooms in the lower level of the Methodist Church in Coupeville are often busy with the activities of a variety of organizations. But rarely as lively as they are from 9 - 11:30 Wednesday, Thursday and Friday mornings. That's when the 3 and 4-year-olds arrive for the Central Whidbey Co-op Preschool.

The 3-year-olds have one "day off," but the 4-year-olds attend school all three days.

The 12 to 15 busy little bodies are guided by three parents (mostly moms) and teacher Cherie Smith.

There are a lot of things to do in 2-1/2 hours - - hands-on activities to build eye and hand coordination; easel and finger painting, arts and crafts, Play Doh, and a table filled with sand or beans or rice which the youngsters manipulate to draw their designs "just right."

There are tapes and books and movement music and a sharing time. When it's time to run, they are taken outside to play ball or perhaps a game of "Red Rover." And, on not so nice days, they have tunnels in the hall to wiggle through.

Active in the community for nearly 20 years, the preschool is rated first class by past members and the 12 families who are current members. They are well informed and like having a part in planning their child's training by helping select the curriculum and assisting in the classroom.

The cooperative requires a parent to volunteer in the classroom a couple of times each month and attend one monthly meeting.

Once a month, Peggy Stanford from Family Life Department of the Skagit Valley College attends the class. She keeps the preschool on track with suggestions on age appropriate activities, discipline, and child development.

Then there is the fund-raising committee.

1997's first fund raiser is from 9 a.m to 3 p.m. Saturday at the Cam-Bey Apartments on North Main. Perhaps you'll find a treasure at the multi-family rummage sale. Proceeds will be used to buy curriculum material and outside playground equipment.

***

***

Why am I always surprised to find links to almost any group of people in our community?

Remember when I asked who "those wonderful little gift boxes" were at the Greening Parade? Well, they were the children from the Central Whidbey Co-op Preschool!

Who else?

By the way, if you decide to register your child for the fall session and check out the preschool first, you just might run into Carrie Ann Walker. You'll know her by her purple "fish hat."

Call Debbie Armstrong at 678-3730 and see what happens.

***

Lillian Huffstetler has a wealth of historical information stored in her memory, on reams of paper and in books she has gathered over a lifetime.

She generously shares all she knows with family members, "So someone will always have the facts."

But history wasn't on Lillian's mind last week. It was all the debris from madronas, "the tree that causes trouble 13 months out of every year" and fir needles..wet fir needles.

Lillian loves the madronas even if they are a problem with falling leaves and berries and bark, but the leavings are full of tannic acid and will sterilize the ground she says, "so the little critters have to be raked up."

She was also a bit irate after reading that the trees had been 'planted' on Madrona Way. They are very difficult to replant and why would anyone plant what's already there?

The wet fir needles are a different matter. They are everywhere and "just part of the joy of living in the woods."

However, as far as she knows, they are of no earthly use so she's looking for a way to market them.

There must be someone out there who'd like to be a millionaire. Do it with fir needles...wet ones.

Lillian will be your chief supplier.

***

Happy Birthday to Rick Fuller, Jane Jones, and Beckie Riecks.

'Green Door' to open over Greenbank Store

March 14, 1997

The minute Sally Coupe Jacobson starts talking about her beloved Greenbank, it comes alive and everything makes sense.

She's the history expert, and as I listened to her, she took me back to the Greenbank of the 1800's. I could *see* a thriving community, the Mosquito ferry, the general store, the post office, the hotel on Wonn Road and Calvin Phillips' 6,000 acre model farm with pigs and cows and loganberries.

The Phillips, founders of Greenbank, advertised the farm nationwide to bring people to Greenbank ... to have a better life.

So it made good sense for Sally and Randy to open *The Green Door Restaurant* in Greenbank for that same purpose. They believe if they serve good, wholesome food, they can bring people to Greenbank and help local suppliers have a better life.

They've already helped. And been helped. Many made donations and local carpenters have been hired.

The Loft restaurant that was above Coupe's Greenbank Store since the 1970's is gone - - completely. Walls were torn down, and windows removed and reset to give diners a spectacular view of Baby Island.

Inside windows are open so the kitchen help can enjoy the same view and visit with customers. In the corner is the cook stove from the Phillips' home.

The bar has disappeared and, in its place, is a huge hearth that Randy built. The hearth holds a green cast iron propane stove modified to burn without heat. Customers can sit on the hearth or on the 1930's davenport facing it and be cozy any time of the year.

Since the Green Door is smoke free, rounded steps built by Ryan lead to French doors for outside dining, and alder wood lights made by Dave Altman in the 1970's with galvanized funnels for globes hang from the ceiling.

There is a window full of green glass pieces, and shelves line the walls to display antique scales, watering cans, and utensils. Bookcases are ready to hold the "harvest of the island" food products, cooking and gardening books and brochures of local businesses.

The screen doors Sally and Randy wanted were out of their price range, so they bought ready-mades, ripped out the screens and inserted scroll work and dowels.

Sally says everyone who sees them wants one. She doesn't have time to make more screen doors, so she told her friend how - - and another local business is off and running.

Every piece of furniture in the restaurant was purchased from antique shops on the island "at good prices from good people interested in helping us succeed." There are round oak tables, butcher block squares and an old patio table in the corner which Sally says will be the best seat in the house for people-watching.

What do the Jacobsons know about the restaurant business? Sally's experience goes back to her senior year when she worked for her uncle at Mindy's Button Willows in Freeland and at Bush Point. She also helped start Pizza Haven in Alderwood Mall.

To learn more, Sally and her mom Mary visited every restaurant on the island and talked to friends in the business, studying menus, prices and people.

Besides, Sally believes running a restaurant isn't really about running a restaurant. She thinks it's about serving your friends and listening to them.

And being real.

They'll be ready to prove that theory in about three weeks when their restaurant opens.

The menu is American using the best recipes of former Loft owners, but with the Jacobson twist. Nothing is prepackaged, everything is made from scratch and fresh — fresh from the farm and fresh from the sea.

The herbs will come from Sally's Sassafras Farm now tended by daughters, Mary and Sarah. Sales, classes, and tours at the farm will continue but wind up with lunch at the Green Door Restaurant.

"It all goes together," Sally said, "the store, the restaurant, Sassafras Farm, the local gardeners, farmers, and craftsmen."

"Others have operated the Greenbank store and the Loft, but they didn't have the Coupe spirit - - that's the difference," she said.

I think she's right.

Just listening to her talk, I could feel the atmosphere and smell the food made from scratch.

I was ready to order lunch!

***

YD Auction a chance to bid on great items, help teens

March 21, 1997

Something wonderful is happening in our community Saturday.

Dozens of friends and neighbors are joining to make the second Youth Dynamics Spring Auction '97 a huge success.

The reasons are simple. Parents and community members want our teenagers to continue to have a place to hold meetings and have scheduled events after football games.

They also want our teenagers to continue to have an opportunity to attend YD sponsored events - - and sometimes that means partial payment assistance is needed.

To raise needed funds, the adult support group holds the November Progressive Dinner and this Saturday evening's Silent Auction.

The YD events are fantastic: *Rendezvous* gives kids a 3-day Memorial weekend at Lake Chelan that includes rock climbing and white water rafting.

The *Polar Bear Expedition* during winter break offers sessions at Hurricane Ridge. The mission is to help students gain self esteem and build character.

And there's *Chill Out* at Mt. Baker with five days of fun ski time.

Chairman Sandey Brandon says she and husband Bob believe in the good that Mike Unruh's YD brings to the young people on Central Whidbey. They believe young people, especially teens, need to be cherished by us all. A lot of people agree with the Brandons and are working hard to keep YD effective and to make the auction a success.

See the impressive list of donors and the donations they've made to the *YD Spring Auction '97* in this issue of *The Coupeville Examiner*. Saturday evening, attend the preview that begins at 5:30 p.m. Then, at 6:30 p.m., start bidding!

Bid for awesome things - - an Elton Bennett original, an overnighter at one of Whidbey's finest B&B's, or enjoy an overnight trip to Vancouver for two that includes train fare & hotel.

Or be practical - - get some legal advice, have your hair or nails done, or bid for custom tractor work to spruce up your yard with crushed rock or top soil.

Or have fun - - join Sheriff Hawley for a "Jailhouse Blues Lunch" or invite all of your friends to Ian Tully's bagpipe recital on Ebey's Bluff.

It's a community auction, so come to the Coupeville Elementary school multipurpose room and enjoy Coupeville graduate Ray Shelley's jazz band, indulge in the extraordinary dessert buffet and bid.

Join your community in cherishing our future.

See you there!

***

Just in time for Easter!

St. Mary's Annual Spring Bake Sale 10 a.m. to 3 p.m. Saturday at the church on North Main in Coupeville. Wonderful baked goods including special breads and desserts. They'll go fast!

An added bonus is a White Elephant sale.

***

What a St. Patrick's Day!

We attended an evening of wonderful "straight from Ireland" music, song and dance at St. Mary, Star of the Sea, in Port Townsend. Harpist Mara Grey opened the program.

Then, for 90 minutes, we sat entranced.

The Irish Planxtey O'Rourke group played toe tapping, hand clapping jigs and reels and we watched Paul turn on his Irish charm as he applied a little duct tape to his disintegrating Elbow Pipe to finish "The Bright Lady."

The five youngsters from County Cork step danced their way right into our hearts..and the singers. Oh, the singers - - a cappella.

Each, including Everett's David McCourt, the man who brought the group and his 11-year-old granddaughter to the United States, stood quietly alone on the stage, then simply raised the microphone and sang.

Old, beautiful, haunting Irish ballads — *The Rare Old Times, Mountains of Mourne, Kevin Barry, A Mother's Love is a Blessing,* and more.

Sitting next to me was Port Townsend resident Elma Beary, who came from Ireland only 16 years ago, softly singing every word...with feeling.

We heard wonderful Irish jokes and were told that the reason the Irish dance with their arms close to their bodies is because the dance floors in Ireland are so very small.

Sounded like blarney to me!

***

My Chelsea, Michigan daughter and my Seattle son are both 39 this month! Wouldn't want to do that again!

Let's all just wear name tags

March 28, 1997

I get so frustrated when I can't put a name on a face I know well and have to ask someone who knows "who that is."

But Saturday was the end.

Twice, I was asked "who is that?" Both times I knew the answer, but neither time could I put a name on the person who was asking me "who that is!" When a fellow said he "liked the article" I did about him, I raced through the alphabet looking for his name.

No luck. He knew I didn't have a clue long before he told me who he was.

My frustration did fade a bit when a woman I've known for 12 years called me *Helen* and it disappeared completely when another called me *Charlene*.

So, I know I'm not alone in this memory thing. But I don't have to like it. I hate it when I can't put names and faces together.

Think about it. In a community this size, people wear many, many hats. You know Bill when he's behind the counter preparing your prescription, but when he's carting chairs around town park for Concerts on the Cove - - are you sure?

We need to help each other. The crazy thing is that we join a club and wear our name tag to the meeting where everyone knows who we are.

The minute we step out of the role people know us in, we take off our name tags and change our shirt. Later, we head for Prairie Center and get miffed when our friend from the club walks right past without a word.

It's nuts!

Give her a break! She's trying to remember who you are.

If I wear a name tag so you know who I am, can I ask you who you are? OK, I'm putting one on.

The rip it off/slap it on name sticker would be fine, but I found something better. It's going to be one of the 15 name tags I found stashed in my *save it* box. They are from every where: Boeing (think I was supposed to turn that in), USO, Dakota County Tribune, Glass Bottle Blowers Association, retreats - - on and on.

They'll work fine, too! Don't you have some from your past? Dig yours out, pin one on and lets swap stories. Not only will we know who we're talking to, we'll share a bit about who we use to be.

Whatever you do, please be kind and put your name right in my face!!

***

If you got a "deal" at the Youth Dynamics' Silent Auction, maybe you missed the whole point. It takes a lot of dollars to pay rent, buy equipment and supplies and help kids who can't swing the entire payment to attend YD events.

Supporters solicited, organized, baked and set up the auction to fill those needs. They did a great job. I hope you dug deep and paid the price. They're our kids too.

I spent a bit more than planned and found it impossible to keep an eye on my bids for favorite items. I was so busy challenging Ron Huff in our vet struggle that I missed out on Sandy D's angel.

Oh, well.

Chairperson Sandey Brandon was thrilled with the community involvement. "Exactly what we had hoped for - - a fun event that included school personnel, business owners, parents, employees and employers, retirees...just about everyone, the response was overwhelming."

***

About Sandey Brandon. Five years ago she and Bob decided to move to Whidbey Island. They already owned the property and knew they wanted to live here forever. They didn't expect to miss California nor that lifestyle, and they don't.

In San Diego, Bob built exhibits at the Museum of Man in Balboa Park, and Sandey managed property and invested pension plans through *Aftermath*, her own corporation. Now, Bob is employed at PS Hair Design, and Sandey, an expert proofreader and copy editor who loves to put words on paper and on shirts, is editing books and doing silk screening.

You can find her *Aftermath* shirts at the Coupeville Harbor Store or, if you can wait, she will be in booth no. 200 at the Coupeville Arts and Crafts Festival in August.

***

May your Easter be blessed and beautiful. And may you find all the colored eggs before the lawn mower does.

Sweet mixture draws hummers

April 4, 1997

Put out your humming bird cocktail!

The hummers are magnificent. We've had eight beauties swarming around our container every day this week. Gordie made the mixture much stronger than usual, and the assemblage is unbelievable!

I am not messing with his recipe.

***

March 11, I found Jack Pour in the Windermere\Center Isle lot on South Main. He had his camera trained on the 1980 Honda Civic Station Wagon perched on Fred Christian's tow truck and Jack had a sad, sad face.

"That's my baby," he said, "I bought her 17 years ago - - when I was stationed in Guam. She's been to Hawaii with me, and for years, she's been serviced regularly at the Honda shop in Mt. Vernon. In November, she had 350K miles and they said she was just like a new car - - with 150K miles to go."

Then, Jack passed his "baby" on to an unnamed person. Six months later, for want of an oil change, it was "Adios, Honda."

That morning, Fred parked his tow truck this way and that way so Jack could take pictures of his "baby," and I did what I could to make the farewell easier. I could understand.

Once upon a time, I had an English car about the size of a small freezer. Before I bought it, it had been involved in a shooting escapade. So, I could park it anywhere in Burien and someone would be waiting for me when I got back to tell me how the bullet holes got in the seat and in the windshield. But it too went to car heaven.

Send Jack a card at the Senior Services of Island County 2845 E Hwy 525 Langley - - if you can appreciate his pain.

***

This year, Easter morning looked very different to the 26 religious education students who had parts in the Passion Play at St. Mary's.

It had been five years since the last Passion Play was performed in the parish, so most of the kids were too young to remember ever seeing it. Yes, they knew the story. Yes, it would be fun to be in a play that had no speaking parts, but they weren't very interested. There were few volunteers, so parts were assigned, and for three Sundays after Mass, the students walked through their parts - - - each time with a little more understanding.

Then on Palm Sunday, as the Gospel was read from the altar, the young actors suddenly "heard" exactly who they were. They recognized the importance of their roles and, at dress rehearsal that day, things were very different. They had definite ideas on what their body language should be. They knew what their character was doing --- and thinking.

Wednesday evening, Pam Robinett and Melissa Baker performed makeup magic, the costumes Annette Potenziani and I had prepared were adjusted and the students were ready.

Jesus, (Jimmy Brown) was spit upon, beaten and humiliated by Centurion Caden Russell and the Roman soldiers Sarah Dugger, John Armendariz and Ian Erwin who carried whips and spears.

Jesus' disciples, Jeremiah Turnek, Clayton Luker and Richard Dugger abandoned Him. He was betrayed by Judas (Thomas Riordan), and denied by Peter (Joe Erwin). Only John (Zack Simonson) remained faithful.

The women of Jerusalem, Cassie Schwenker and Jessica Armendariz wept and stayed close to Jesus' mother, (Maria Hartshorn), Mary Magdalene (Bronwyn Russell) and Veronica, (Erin Riordan).

Those in power, dressed in silks and laden with jewelry, judged unjustly or assumed no responsibility in the decisions: Pilate (Adam Wood), his wife (Cavan Simonson), and their servant, Kelly Ess; High Priest Joe Rojas, his servant Andrea Brown; and King Herod (Brian Baker) and his servant Whitney Clark.

The lights were low and there were no sounds in St. Mary's except for lector Joe McGraw reading the scriptures, the crack of the whip, the pounding of the nails. And the marvelous voice of Richard Hartshorn singing "Were You There?"For 30 minutes the students *were there* and they took the entire church community with them. It was awesome.

Yes, Easter morning did look different this year.

Directors Jane Desmond and Bud Dorr and coordinators Florence Dorr, Cathy Russell, and Janet Rojas won't have any trouble getting volunteers for next years' production.

The kids are ready.

***

May 4, Concerts on the Cove presents the Municipal Choir of Pozo Almonte and the Seattle Peace Chorus at the Performing Arts Center at Coupeville High School. Tickets at Coupeville Pharmacy, Wind & Tide Bookshop in Oak Harbor, Book Bay in Freeland, JB's Ice Creamery and Espresso, Langley and Whidbey CyberC@fe in Clinton. Or Call 678-4684. Don't miss it!

'Nothing but Net' nothing but great

April 11, 1997

Next time you shop at Prairie Center or stop at Videoville, take a closer look.

Your counterman may be Mike Lodell the star of *Nothing But Net* or writer and director David Svien.

A spoof on *Hoop Dreams,* it's a goofy, fun 22 minute video starring Mike as Jimmy Valentine, a no-talent basketball player who sees himself as the next great find of the NBA.

Jimmy *knows* he will be discovered - - probably behind the counter at Big Bertha's Meat and Vegie Mart where he works as a bag boy. If not as a bag boy, for sure in the upcoming Big City 101 Tournament.

At 28, Jimmy trusts his natural talent and his unpatented "right handed lay-up" to take him to the top.

In *Nothing But Net,* a lot of things happen in 22 minutes.

Jimmy is fired by Big Bertha (Christy Tingstad) for shooting baskets in the back room. He's interviewed by Louise Walton (Miriam Meyer) who gives him a job working with youngsters Spenser Meckley, Nick, Sarah & Mikall Marley, who quickly drive him off.

And he loses beaucoup bucks to Megan & Kathryn Meyer when he tries to beat them at shooting baskets.

Preparing for the tournament, Jimmy concocts a green energy mix which lays him low. He recovers just in time to compete. Now, everyone gets into the act. Jimmy's first two challengers are eliminated — B.C. Wells as Lyle the Dancing Assassin, runs into a steel post.

To the rescue comes the WGH ambulance with paramedics Ian Tully and Alanna Hutchinson who are on time, but less than honest.

When Cardiac Arrest played by Quentin Youderian is attacked by a "stranger," Jimmy prepares to challenge his last hurdle to the NBA, Joe the Shark played by Joe Meyer.

The rest you have to see for yourself.

I enjoyed every one of the 22 minutes. There are some very good lines and Jimmy's look of amazement at sinking a ball and his shifty eyed wonder at the attack on Cardiac Arrest were great.

And I'm impressed with David's ability to guide 15 people through 22 minutes of action.

Noah Lodell played young Jim, Amanda Bentley played Becky Kersey, Sarah Svien did costumes, Bob Fasolo as high school coach Dexter Ramsey, who thought "Jimmy had lots of spunk, but no talent," and Rebecca Lodell catered the troops.

Nothing But Net, produced with Johnathon Young, is David's second short film. When Miramax Films held a "life in a video store" contest for video store employees across the U.S., David wrote and directed a seven-minute silent feature on the "worst customer in the world" starring Chad Jones and Jennifer Meyer.

He won first place!

David and Mike expect to do more films, hopefully movies with better equipment. David is working on a full-length feature film and scripts. Mike is thinking about auditioning for theater. Both are anxious to get on with their dreams.

In the meantime, Mike is a checker at Prairie Center Grocery and David manages Videoville on South Main and writes *Reel Time* for *The Coupeville Examiner*.

David says *Nothing But Net* was a low budget, fun video, and if anyone wants to borrow it over night, it's available from Videoville on South Main.

Get it, it's fun!

***

Ran into Vicki Staley and Dolores Fresh in Langley last week. Its been a long time since we've seen our friend Dolores. Once upon a time, Dolores owned The Victorian B&B in Coupeville, and was President of the Central Whidbey Chamber of Commerce.

On my desk is the "brick" Dolores created for the January 19, 1990 chamber installation dinner. She encouraged involvement and, through her optimism and faith in Coupeville, doubled the chamber's membership during her term.

Now she lives on the south end and besides subbing at South Whidbey Intermediate School, she heads her pet project, the *Red Flyer Reading Club*. Developed by Dolores, the "Club" brings together volunteers and children who read to each other on a regular basis.

Sounds like Dolores.

***

If it's for the community, chances are, Ken's there

April 18, 1997

"It's about time everybody knew what Ken Hofkamp's up to."

That's what I keep hearing about this guy at Prairie Center. The same phrases keep coming up - - like: *unsung hero, always there to help, all around nice guy.*

Soroptimist International of Coupeville sings his praises for donating 90 dozen eggs to their '97 Easter egg hunt. Ken's always been there when their organization needed help, but eggs were new.

The Lions' white canes, the Girl Scouts cookies, the elementary school soup label box — all important to community members are important to Ken too.

Carol Lee Hershman will tell you that. The 1996 Senior Class brunch benefited from Ken's generosity, as have other classes since 1972. "The World's Largest Banana Split," an after-game event wouldn't have happened without him. And mention fridge space, ice cream, pop, auction, and the kids in YD know "Ken did it."

"It's not just product that Ken donates," says Jacquie Vincent, "it's his time and his faith in our kids. Half of the kids in Coupeville have worked at Prairie Center....and he never loses faith in them."

Sandey Brandon calls it Ken's "soft spot for kids." Whatever it is, it works.

Seems if it's for the community, Ken's there.

In fact, if you add all of the above with his service in the Central Whidbey Chamber of Commerce, and almost every other organization on Central Whidbey, and his help to people of every age, he covers a *lot* of community.

I think that's it. If you want to know what community is, follow Ken Hofkamp around. He knows what it is because he *is* community.

***

Fran Einterz can tell you a story about the importance of kids wearing helmets - - and of men staying in shape.

***

***

Some very important little people helped me over the edge, and on April 15th I began my sixth week as a non-smoker. Not bad!

No coughing - - more time. Only one shower a day instead of one in the morning and one before I leave home so I don't offend anyone by smelling smoky.

Downside? I am so thirsty. I've gained a little weight...all right *quite a little*. Actually, it's a good thing I'm wearing my name tag.

I tried to quit many times over the 47 years I smoked, but, to tell you the truth, I couldn't. The quit-smoking gum burned my mouth, I failed the Boeing classes, and once I even climbed on a chair, put my cigarettes on top of the hutch, then resolutely put the chair back by the table.

Told myself I could have a cigarette anytime I wanted to, but I had to go get the chair and climb up to get one every time. Didn't slow me down a bit, I just spent a lot of time lugging that chair back and forth.

I could write a book! I don't mean to make light of it. Well, maybe I do. I am so thankful that it's over - - that I'm free - - that I have a hard time being somber.

It helps that Gordie's 50-plus pipes haven't been touched since Dec. 1, 1995. That's the day he had his second emergency bypass. He complains loudly now and then, but his pipe rack is getting dustier every day.

We are grateful.

***

The Vracins are back from Hawaii tanned and rested. For the first time, they spent the entire vacation on Oahu. Loved it!

***

Our community has been diminished by the death of Louise Reed. Louise was very active in Coupeville and in Oak Harbor for many years and will be missed.

***

Rev. Al and Liz Waln are moving to Des Moines, Washington. They will be honored at a special potluck and farewell program this Sunday at the Coupeville United Methodist Church where Al served as pastor from 1968 until he retired in 1984. The many friends the Walns made in the church and in the community are invited to attend the potluck immediately after the 11:00 am service.

Come, wish them well.

***

Happy Birthday, Cathy Russell, Happy 21st, grandson Rob Workman!

Volunteering can open up new doors

April 25, 1997

You can't join every group, but if you want to meet nice people, there are a lot of opportunities out there.

This month, two of our most dynamic organizations are actively seeking new members.

The Coupeville Festival Association and Concerts on the Cove are gearing up for their summer activities and need not only dollar support, but also volunteers with time, energy, and ideas.

CFA is preparing for the 34th Coupeville Arts and Crafts Festival August 9 and 10, and COC begins the summer series of Sunday afternoon concerts in town park on July 20.

If you hurry, you could even help COC with the Municipal Choir of Pozo Almonte, Chile on May 4. Membership does take some of your time, but it's exciting to be part of a group doing good things.

If you're new in town, or just want to do something wonderful, go to a meeting, meet the people, and you'll be hooked.

Check out the Coupeville Festival Association by calling Volunteer Coordinator Mary Jo Isenmann 678-2064 or call Concerts on the Cove at 678-4684.

***

Our grandson Rob was living with us when Ellen Slater was writing her column for Oak Harbor's *Whidbey News-Times,* and sometimes it was the only thing that got us through some problems that, at the time, we thought were huge.

Ellen, in her witty way could lighten up the whole thing by writing about her twin daughters Natalie and Marissa, who were the same age as Rob, being involved in a similar "problem."

Ellen's husband Scott, the girls and their friends were really what the column was about. Reading it, we watched a whole group of kids grow up.

We celebrated Rob's 21st birthday Sunday, and I wondered how the twins were doing.

Ellen says they are fine. Better than fine. Natalie is in her last year at Skagit Valley College and will continue, probably in Seattle, to earn her elementary teacher certification.

Marissa attended SVC and worked at Sears in the auto department where she found her love — mechanical work. She works in Everett in an on-the-job training program where she's learning to become a licensed aircraft mechanic.

Ellen also says the girls are now beautiful young women. "It has been such a pleasure to watch them grow and mature into wonderful adults," she said.

And Ellen and Scott?

Well, Scott's job remains the same, but Ellen is working in Everett at Acrowood, a company with a 100-year history in heavy equipment for pulp and paper mills. She rides the bus some days and the ferry every day and finds it "a whole other world."

"I've met wonderful people," she said, "especially 10-year-old Seth, who goes to school over there and likes me." Sometimes Ellen has trouble convincing him it's OK for him to "sit by strangers" when she and Seth can't sit together.

Seth makes commuting easy.

Ellen still has migraine headaches caused by her accident on Highway 20 almost 4 years ago. (we saw the accident - - cars were lined up for at least a half mile.) The headaches are not as bad as they were, but bad enough for her to try acupuncture. It helps.

Scott and Ellen have their house on the market. When it sells, they'll build in Kineth Point.

"Selling a house is a lot of work," Ellen said. "We've painted and cleaned and the yard looks better than it ever has. Now we have to pretend we don't live here and keep it in perfect condition for showing."

Ellen's life is good. She likes her job and is learning to balance it all - - to take advantage of why they live on the island and commute to work every day.

Although she did a feature for the Coupeville Arts Center in the March/April issue of *Fiberarts*, Ellen doesn't have time to write any more.

It's her only disappointment in life.

I'm disappointed too. I miss her column.

***

Five of my Grand Forks families lost their homes this week.

Basements full of water to the first and second floors. They are all with family in Williston today, but are anxious to go home as soon as possible.

They are all safe. I hope yours are too.

Island awash with song, blooms Sunday

May 2, 1997

Invitations are out for May 4, a Sunday to remember, and you can have it all!

Kristi O'Donnell of Meerkerk Rhododendron Gardens, invites you to come see the beautiful Greenbank Fairy Princess at their Mayflower Garden Party, and Vern Olsen, of Concerts on the Cove invites you to come enjoy the lively music and dance of Northern Chile and the Andes performed by the Municipal Chorus of Pozo Almonte and the Seattle Peace Chorus at the CHS Performing Arts Center.

There is a bit of one-up-manship between Kristi and Vern.

"The Princess," Kristi says, "carries a magic wand, has petticoats made from flower petals, woven silks and spider webs, and she wears golden slippers and a flowery halo on her flowing, glowing red hair."

"The music of Pozo Almonte and the Seattle Peace Chorus," Vern said, "is magnificent - - especially the presentation of the Misa de la Cruz, del Sur - - the Mass of the Southern Cross. Each movement of the folk mass, composed by Vincente Bianchi, is based on a popular South American dance rhythm."

"Well," said Kristi, "the Fairy Princess and members of the Greenbank Garden Club will help the children understand how to make magical wands, weave paper baskets, string necklaces of rhodo florets, even decorate a halo with flowers from Mary Petry's Flower Farms."

"Fine," Vern said, "but as Les Asplund said,'children need to understand the Chilean people who are as friendly as anyone can be'. Yes, a little basic Spanish is nice, but a smile will go a long, long way." Les, who doesn't speak much Spanish spent three weeks in Chile with Vern and the Peace Chorus in 1995.

Kristi invites children of all ages to dance around the Maypole while Talia Marcus performs musical magic on her fiddle, or to hike the five mile nature trail thru the woodland preserve or just enjoy the 10 acres of gardens in full bloom. All beautiful.

There are lots of signs to Meerkerk Gardens just south of Greenbank off State Highway 525.

Vern invites you to come to the concert and meet the men and women who left Pozo Almonte, the town some had never been away from. They traveled thousands of miles to the United States, a country they had only heard about, to sing and dance for us, here in Coupeville.

We may not understand Spanish, but we are all experts when it comes to magnificent music, beautiful dancing, and wonderful people.

Tickets at Coupeville Pharmacy and at the door.

Yes, you can have it all! Go to the party and enjoy - - then on to the concert!!

1 to 4 p.m. Meerkerk Rhododendron Garden's Sunday Garden Party

3 to 5 p.m. Concerts on the Cove's Municipal Chorus of Pozo Almonte and the Seattle Peace Chorus.

***

While looking for information about the Greenbank Garden Club, I found some other stories — too many for this issue.

Peggy Berg was one.

Peggy knows a lot about the Garden Club, she's been a member ever since she and Russ moved to Whidbey 34 years ago.

Both Northwesterners, Peggy was from Richmond Beach and Russ from Edmonds. As a John Deere Representative, they moved to Yakima then to Whittier, California. They loved Whittier. The city retains the Quaker influence and "that," Peggy said, "was something we really needed with three teen-age daughters."

In the early 60's, the Bergs knew they had to come back to the Northwest. They wanted property on the water and needed a shop for Russ's dream - - a business of his own.

During their search, the Bergs stopped at the Greenbank store and saw an elderly gentleman across the street struggling with his lawn mower. They asked if he would be interested in selling, and yes, Mr. Lucas would sell.

So the Bergs moved to Whidbey Island in 1964 and Russ opened his repair shop.

They wouldn't live anywhere else, but two of their daughters stayed in California, one in San Clemente and one in Yorba Linda. The other daughter lives in Edmonds.

"We have six grandchildren,"Peggy said, "five grandsons and one granddaughter - - our princess - - and six great grandchildren."

They have a fantastic vegetable garden, but Peggy had knee surgery and can't work outside like she wants to. "I was the flower lady forever, now I just can't do as much. "One thing though, "Peggy says, "the lilacs are blooming and it's spring and I love it."

Yes!

A little Bunny Hop, a little Hokey Pokey

May 9, 1997

No doubt, members of the Seattle Peace Chorus and the Chilean singers left Coupeville with more than a song in their hearts.

Sunday afternoon, the two groups performed to a packed house with the audience toe tapping and swaying to the music. The instant they finished each song, every person sprang to their feet as one, cheering and clapping.

Again, a standing ovation for the special performances by individual musicians. Monday morning, Coupeville high school students repeated both ovations.

Sunday evening, Concerts on the Cove served dinner at the recreation hall for the performers, their overnight hosts, and Mayor Nancy Conard, who was presented with mementos from Chile at the concert.

The dinner went fine and if a language barrier existed, it was hard to tell with all the laughing and talking. Certainly there was no barrier during the dancing. Vern Olsen played his accordion and everyone danced the Bunny Hop and the Hokey Pokey.

The whole event was wonderful.

Hats off to Concerts on the Cove and the entire community for joining together in an effort that produced unbelievable results!

If you want to know who did what, call 678-4684 and request a "who dunnit" sheet.

***

Our Coupeville kids are doing something great again!

Under the direction of drama teacher Wendy Organ, 13 of our young people have practiced for two months to present Agatha Christie's *Ten Little Indians*.

Performances are at 7 p.m. May 8, 9, and 10 at the Performing Arts Center and they are free.

Refreshments will be available and donations gladly accepted to offset royalty fees.

Don't miss seeing the young actors, Josh Butela, Leah Harrison, Mike Losert, Tony Moore, Doug Boling, Dan Russell, Jeff Bass, Joanna Thome, Leslie McDougall, Ian Stone, and Brie Sword. And the work of stage manager, Joe Bass and sound and light technician, Evan Parker.

***

This is Kristi O'Donnell's fourth season as manager at Greenbank's Meerkerk Rhododendron Gardens.

Kristi and her husband Keith met in Cincinnati where they both taught at colleges. She taught floral design and served as horticulturist with the Cincinnati Park Board and Keith taught classical guitar. They combined their interests, flowers and music, and brought it all to Whidbey Island in 1993.

Actually, in 1990, they came to visit friends in Seattle. Turned out schedules were skewed and they came too early, so they went camping in the mountains. They fell in love..with the water, the mountains, the rhodies, the butterflies.

In December 1992, Kristi dreamed about rhodies and the next spring, as members of the American Association of Botanical Gardens & Arboreta, they received word the Seattle Rhododendron Society was advertising for a Manager at Meerkerk Gardens.

Kristi was chosen over twenty other applicants.

The special events planned for the 1997 season at the Gardens are proof the AABGA made the right choice. This Saturday, wear purple, and you'll win a plant. Sunday, enjoy a Mother's Day concert. On May 17, there's a Garden Party Benefit for Hospice.

Besides keeping the Meerkerk Gardens beautiful, Kristi is active in our community. A member of the *Greenbank Community Council,* she worked hard to stop the DOT park-and-ride plans for Hancock Lake and is vice president of the *Friends of Whidbey Island* the organization spearheading the Saving of Greenbank Farm project.

Call Kristi at 678-5736 to be involved.

***

For almost two years, Irene and Ernie Gendron have been active at St. Marys, enjoyed swinging with the Whidbey Whirlers, and made a lot of friends. They love spending time with Coupeville daughter and son-in-law Lisa & Richard Dugger and their grandchildren Richard 9, and Sarah, 13. But Irene and Ernie are going home back to Pittsburgh, Pennsylvania, where Irene lived all her life.

"I'm just too lonesome to stay any longer," she said.

A lot of people will welcome them home in July, including her sisters, four children, nine grandchildren and two great-grandchildren and the Wolf Rockers Square Dance Club.

They'll be missed here.

Zigging, zagging on her way to doctorhood

May 16, 1997

Sometimes, even when you know where you're going, it takes a long time to get there.

Wendy McDonald knew she'd be a doctor when she was in kindergarten ....maybe an internist, maybe a surgeon.

Few family members took her seriously, and those who did, tried to convince her what she really wanted to be was a nurse.

This month, her family will attend her graduation from the University of New Mexico and she'll be on her way to Boise, Idaho for an internship in internal medicine. It's the last step on a long road.

Wendy's schooling has been a series of stops and starts. But she proves a little zigging and zagging on the way is fine, as long as you keep going.

In addition to her degree from the U of NM, she has a bachelor's degree from St. John's, a Liberal Arts College in Santa Fe. For a couple of years she majored in physics and a couple of times, she dropped out.

But she's almost there.

Her first attempt at attending a college, was in Colorado, and it was disastrous. Coming from a small high school in El Paso, she was overwhelmed. She quit school and traveled, working now and then.

For a while, after entering New Mexico State University at Las Cruces, she crammed as many classes as possible into two days a week and skied the other five. But then she fell in love with physics and spent two years there.

Her best year? Wendy spent her rotation year in Alaska. She loved Ketchikan, the doctors, the patients, the town's people.

"Ketchikan," she said, "is a magical place. I felt good just being there."

Being on call 24 hours a day, she admits, was hard. "But I really learned." Wendy took a couple afternoons off for sightseeing. One day she visited the fjords, the other she went on a boating trip, during which she saw all the wild life she ever dreamed of seeing.

When the year was over, she spent three months, "the best time of my life," in Baton Rouge with her brother. While there, she worked in a Cajun pub.

Wendy completed her studies in New Mexico, then spent 18 months in Coupeville, studying for her boards, connecting with family, cooking at Rosi's Garden, and doing research on youth violence at the UW.

She says it was "the second best time of her life."

And she still thinks about being a surgeon.

Changing, Wendy said, is the notion surgeons must be tough as nails, must learn to be *above it all*, and must believe they are immune to every disease and injury known to man.

In other words, godlike.

"Today, it's OK for surgeons to be human beings," Wendy said.

Some surgeons have always understood that, including two she knows in Coupeville, her father being one of them. She may still follow in his footsteps.

And she's sure she'll return to Ketchikan someday. And she'll come back to Washington, not just to visit her parents, Herb and Susan McDonald, but to enjoy backpacking at Stehekin near Lake Chelan.

"It's so beautiful," she said, "something everyone should go do at least once."

Wendy's ideas seem right...follow your dream and have fun.

***

One year ago next month, Heidi Hennessey and Simon Bargh took over Rosi's Garden Restaurant.

They still own it, but George Sasso is the chef.

Heidi and Simon are too busy with their newest endeavor, the extensive remodeling and the reopening of Christopher's Restaurant and Front Street Cafe. Walls have come down, the works of local artists has gone up, there's a new dance floor and more seating.

Come see them at the grand opening Friday. Hors d'oeuvres are from 5-7 p.m. At 8:30, John Tristao of Creedence Clearwater Revisited fame, and his band start playing.

Good job, Heidi and Simon!

***

The Penn Cove Water Festival gets bigger and bigger. This year there's even a benefit concert at 8:00 p.m. Friday at the high school - - a sea shanty extravaganza with lots of songs to make you laugh and maybe even shed a tear or two.

***

Happy Birthday, Mary Martha Piazzon!

Call it kismet: they knew this was home

May 23, 1997

Annie Horton saw the big blue house with the white fence just south of Greenbank in June when she and her husband came to see if Whidbey would be a good place to retire.

"I'd like to live in a house like that." she told Ross.

The Hortons returned in February and described their dream house to their Realtor and were given a list of 6 possibles. The blue house was the fourth one on the list.

They never saw the fifth.

"We walked in and we were home," Annie said, "we knew this was it."

A police officer in the Santa Clara, California area for 30 years, Ross wasn't quite ready to retire, but Annie moved into the blue house for Thanksgiving 1993. Ross came in January.

They plunged into the community. Neighbors Don and Jan Allen took them to the Rhododendron Society meeting. They joined. Irene Knudson took Annie to the Greenbank Garden Club, she joined. Ross joined Beach Watchers, Annie volunteered at WAIF's thrift store in Freeland. They've had parts in Langley's Murder Mystery weekend and are involved with the Penn Cove Water, during which Ross helps with the canoe races and Annie is involved with the children's craft activities. She is also Meerkerk's beautiful Fairy Princess at the Mayflower Garden Party.

Annie and Ross love the history of their property. They have the Abstract of Title to Lands in Island County, granted in 1872 to the State of Washington by President Ulysses S. Grant. So they know they are the third owners of the house built by Victor Magnusson in 1929. They know Edee Magnusson, Victor and Carrie's daughter, inherited the house and sold it to the previous owners, Eric and Nancy Peterson, in 1986.

The Petersons updated the house, so whenever the Hortons wonder how a nook or cranny was used in the olden days, they call their dentist, Frank Ploof. Dorothy, Frank's mom, and Edee Magnusson were friends and Frank spent a lot of time at the house as a child. He always has an answer.

Annie learned more about the history of their home through the Greenbank Garden Club books. After she joined the club, her hand kept going up whenever something had to be written, so now she's the Scribe and is in charge of all the yearbooks.

It's a fascinating collection and she's learned Victor Magnusson's wife Carrie was one of the founding members of the club and that Edee became a member one year before Annie Zeller Horton was born.

"We just seem to belong to this house, the Garden Club, the whole community," Annie said.

The garage the Hortons built fits perfectly with other outside buildings, and the new picket fence looks like it's been there forever, as do the additions they've made to the porches. In fact, everything fits. The family heirlooms they brought from California, the pieces they've found at local shops, and personal items — right down to Annie's music boxes and even her *little* boxes — all fit perfectly.

So do the hatracks and the armoire that holds costumes from the two years she worked under contract with the California Actors Theatre.

After the theatre closed, Annie was press officer on California's Mediterranean fruit fly eradication project. When that was completed, she was hired to head the fire safety education program for Santa Clara.

Annie's boss, the fire marshal, invited Ross, the police arson investigator, to "come see who's doing the safety job." Ross came, he met Annie, and the couple celebrate that day, February 28, as well as their wedding anniversary.

I must go back to the blue house. I know the stories about the dogs, the sheep, and the antique cars, but I'm still a little fuzzy about Annie's artistic talents.

***

Nice to see Bud Dorr standing on his own two feet again. Bud had an "unfortunate accident" on the golf course months ago and has been wearing a cast and walking ever so carefully with the help of crutches and, more recently, a cane.

Take care, Bud.

***

Congratulations to Director Wendy Organ and the Coupeville High School drama class for their production of *Ten Little Indians*. The cast held us in the palm of their hands throughout the play, and in the end, their believability brought everyone in the audience to the edge of their seats.

Well done!

***

Smiling easy for banker Fakkema

May 30, 1997

Starting Monday, Keith Fakkema won't be the first person you see when you enter Coupeville's InterWest Bank any more. On June 9, after 13 years as branch manager, he moves to InterWest's main office in Oak Harbor as administrative assistant to senior Vice President Scott Southwick.

And you are invited to help Keith celebrate 25 years of service with InterWest Bank from 4 - 6 p.m. Friday, May 30 at the Coupeville Recreation Hall.

Keith's change in position is partly due to the health restrictions resulting from his 10-year struggle with multiple sclerosis.

"To be really effective," Keith said, "a branch manager needs to visit Realtors in their offices and to travel to building sites. I move much too slowly now, and it's time to leave."

An Oak Harbor native, Keith graduated from high school in 1960. He went to college and shared classes in economics and business at Seattle Pacific University with a young lady named Hope.

Today, Hope calmly says she "chased him until he caught me." When he did, they married in Tacoma the day after graduation from SPU on June 6.

"Who," Hope asks, "but a couple of crazy college kids would add the stress of a wedding to the stress of finals!"

That was 33 years ago.

Keith's career in banking began after Hope applied for a job with the Pacific National Bank of Seattle. The interviewer told her she was perfect for the job, but added, "We don't hire women at that level of banking."

Hope went home and told Keith about this great job. "He applied, and it was his," she said.

Keith spent a year of his Army days in Korea, and when he returned, he settled into working for the National Bank of Washington, now called Pacific National Bank.

"I was sure I'd have to wait until I retired before I could return to Whidbey Island," he said. But, after they were in Seattle for 10 years, the Oak Harbor InterWest had an opening. In June 1972, they came home.

Keith remained at the Oak Harbor office until he became the first Coupeville branch manager in 1984.

"Keith was here from the very beginning," assistant branch manager Suzanne Hoel said, "I started a couple years later, and it's been a real pleasure to work with a person who is truly first class in everything he does."

Helping people reach their goal is Keith's favorite part of banking.

"It's meeting the needs of an individual," he said, "going through the process — watching their house go up — seeing it to completion. It's a complicated and cumbersome process, but it's fun and very rewarding."

"The years I've spent in Coupeville have been pure joy," Keith said, "It's tough to leave so many friends behind. I have enjoyed the people immensely, and although I've never lived right in Coupeville, I appreciate the fact that I've been able to work here and be a part of the Coupeville community."

So what changes?

After a week of vacation, Keith will be at his desk in Oak Harbor facing new challenges. Hope will continue her home-based business, *Hope Fakkema Interior Designs*.

And, if Keith really reduces his work hours, they'll spend more time with their beautiful granddaughters, the joy of their lives, Ellen and Claire ages 8 and 25 months.

I know I could get many, many testimonials, but I want to tell you our personal experience with Keith.

We didn't know it then, but, in 1985, when we bought our house in Teronda West, Keith Fakkema had been the InterWest branch manager in Coupeville for only one year.

We were involved in real estate and construction in Seattle, and our experience with banks there was not fun.

Gordon and I walked into Coupeville's InterWest, met Keith Fakkema, did what we had to do, signed our names, shook hands and we were out of there.

Country Cottage Gifts on Front Street...same thing. Like magic!

Yes, Keith does move slower than he did in 1985, but one thing hasn't changed. His smile. When I asked him about that, Keith's voice became even more cheerful and he said "Oh, smiling? That's easy."

I like that guy. We'll all miss him.

***

Rules every child should know

June 6, 1997

Celie, Marvin, Fizzgig and Rufus are just silly looking puppets, but they had the undivided attention of Coupeville's first and second graders. Meanwhile puppeteers, Suzie DuPuis, Carla Roberts, and Rob Dow, taught the students some very important rules.

Rules kids must know to protect themselves from abuse.

"Child sexual abuse is hard to spot - - abusers are so clever," said Jo Gerhard, script writer and moderator of the program, *All About Life*.

"As adults, we have all the rules down," she said. "Kids don't know what the rules are until we teach them - - and then teach them again." That's what the puppet theater does. It's produced by Citizens Against Domestic and Sexual Abuse, and in its second year.

The program gently reinforces what many parents have told their children about what is OK and not OK, and what to do when things don't feel good. Youngsters were reminded that their private parts are exactly that - - private parts where no one should touch them. Our youngsters learned that their private parts are the parts of their body covered by their bathing suit.

Now they know what the words mean.

Rule No.1, Jo told the students, is to "pay attention to your feelings." That means to recognize the difference between good and bad feelings and that your feelings are right!

"How would that make you feel?" Jo asked when puppets Celie and Marvin, a girl and a boy the students' age, were covered with huge kisses from their pet dog Rufus. The children giggled and agreed that their dogs' slobbers or cats' licks feel good.

But, when Marvin was pinched and covered with huge kisses by a relative, the children didn't like that feeling. None of them like being hit or touched or punched or pinched by anyone, even family members or close friends. Sometimes, people who really love kids do things that give children bad feelings.

Sometimes, they don't know; sometimes, they don't care.

Rule No. 2, the children learned, is "say 'No!'" to any uncomfortable touching or scary situations.

"You need to stop bad feelings," to say "*Stop!*" or "*Go away!*" Jo told them. She explained to the kids they could be in danger if someone says, "don't tell anyone," or "this is our secret," or "your mom said come with me." You must say "*No*!" and run. If you can't run, yell!

Rule No. 3, they were told, is "ask an adult to help them when things don't feel good." Jo told them to choose someone they trust. If that person doesn't help, then keep asking for help until someone does.

When Fizzgig, who has several roles in the puppet theater, played a babysitter who promised Marvin a very special treat in exchange for doing a "secret thing," the children shouted warnings to Marvin to say "No!"

And they cheered when he told his mother about the sitter.

Sitting on the floor, the students watched the puppets act out situations the children could, and sometimes do, find themselves in. They giggled at the antics of the puppets and waved their hands to share ideas on how to "tell people who make them feel bad to go away."

Then it was over, and they joined in a song with the puppets.

The song, *I Know What To Do*, had a simple verse, but said it all: "*I know what to do - - I know how I feel - - I say no - - and I ask for help.*"

Can we really teach our children to be safe?

I don't know, but thanks to Citizens Against Domestic and Sexual Abuse, Coupeville's first and second graders have a better chance to avoid being victims.

Jo hopes to expand the program to middle school next year.

Puppeteers are needed.

The requirements are easy and the rewards are terrific. Altho any performing arts experience is a plus, none is necessary. Volunteers must be available during the school day.

And, if you have a silly voice, you'd be perfect.

Call CADA 675-2232.

***

Happy Birthday Krista.
Happy Anniversary Keith and Hope Fakkema.

Fish for fun and prizes — all for very good causes

June 13, 1997

Central Whidbey Lions Club is putting on a Salmon Derby, and it's happening this Saturday and Sunday, June 14 and 15.

Each day, for a $10 ticket, you will be eligible to catch the biggest salmon or the biggest bottom fish and qualify for the big bucks.Top prize is $1,000, second, $300, and third, $200. Weigh-ins will be in the lot next to the Tyee Restaurant on South Main in Coupeville.

Saturday's deadline is 6 p.m. and Sunday's deadline is 2 p.m. Prizes will be awarded for both days at a ceremony on Sunday after the final weigh-in.

Youngsters are encouraged to go fishing with their parents, but those under 15 qualify only for prizes in the youth division. There is a youth first prize of $50.

You don't fish, so why should you buy a ticket? Well, because your numbered ticket could be drawn - - you don't have to be there - - and you may win one of many prizes. All of them are worth much more than the cost of the $10 ticket — from $300 depth finders to ice chests.

But, that's not the best part.

The best part is that all of the money you pay for your tickets goes to good causes...good causes right here in Central Whidbey. Throughout the year, the 38 members of the Central Whidbey Lions Club touch many lives in our community.

At the Coupeville Elementary Halloween Carnival, their darts and balloons booth is a favorite. And, at Christmas and Thanksgiving, dozens of families enjoy a holiday dinner because of the food baskets provided by the Central Whidbey Lions. Last year, each basket contained a week's worth of food thanks to the club's food fund and to members like Ken Hofkamp who donated a huge portion of the basket's contents. Besides the Carnival and the food baskets, club members sell white canes on Sight Days. Every cent goes for better vision. They keep our world cleaner by removing litter on the highway, at Lookout Park on Engle Road, and at Keystone Spit, and they've built handicap ramps at private residences.

Syd Glover, the current "Tail Twister," describes the Central Whidbey Lions Club as a small, *hands-on club*. "We meet at the Tyee for lunch twice a month," Syd said, "and concentrate on one fund-raiser a year. Last year, we raffled off a garden shed. This year, it's the 1st Annual Central Whidbey Lions Salmon Derby."

Getting ready for the derby has been something, Syd said, "We're still receiving donations, and last week Don Piercy, Neil Amtmann, and I and our 'consultants', David Wells and Pat Dozier, were out there 'landscaping' the vacant lot for derby contestant parking and weigh-in."

Syd hopes this is the first of many fishing derbies, and there's a good chance he's right. The Lions already have a full page of things to do different next year, and that's always a good sign.

Tickets are available at Prairie Center Family Grocer, Tyee Restaurant, Hole in the Wall, Ace Hardware in Freeland and in Oak Harbor, Flower's Marine, the Coronet Bay Store, Oak Harbor Marine and Holiday Sports in Burlington.

The price is right, the prizes are great and the money helps you and your neighbors.

***

Julia Hodson was one of the three University of Washington volunteers recently honored as Outstanding Volunteer of the Year. Julia has served on the Foundation for International Understanding through Students for 37 years and has housed and fed dozens of students in her Ledgewood home during that time.

Congratulations, Julia.

***

By the time this goes to press, Gordie and I will be back from Bandon, Oregon.

Wait a minute, I've said that before. Last September, in fact. Well, we are going again although I don't know why. It's so beautiful right here. The sunset last night - - last Friday to you - - was magnificent, and it was right there off the deck. My peonies have exploded, the clematis vines are covered with beauty and the garden needs weeding.

But we are going and we will again walk for miles and miles on Bandon's beautiful beach and stare for hours at Face Rock and keep trying to see the Cat and her Kittens.

We'll go to Old Town for breakfast and go into every shop on every street just to be sure everything is still there where it belongs.

And then we'll come home. Where we belong.

***

Trimmings from old maple won't be going to waste

June 20, 1997

Last Saturday, Petty Officer Second Class Ken Poteet performed a community service in Coupeville.

Ken, who grew up in the tree removal business in St. Louis, Missouri, trimmed and removed dead branches and improved the health of the huge maple in front of Wylie Vracin's office on North Main.

The tree, a bit thinner, but feeling much better, thank you, doesn't look much different than it did 60-plus years ago, says Marilyn Libbey Bailey.

And Marilyn knows. She's lived here all her life and knows a lot about Coupeville and the area around Dr.Vracin's maple tree. Just down the street, next to DJ's Diner, is Marilyn's great-grandfather's home, the *Joseph Barstow Libbey* house, where her father Joe W., his brothers Jessie and Harold and his sister Esther grew up.

The fourth Libbey generation - - Marilyn's - - settled in a couple blocks away in 1934 between the Joseph W. Libbey house and where the maple stood. Just a wee one when her father and mother, Joe W. and Ethel Hancock Libbey, built their home, Marilyn and her siblings, Wayne, Lyla Snover, Janice Coffman, and Leland, walked past that tree every day on their way to school. Today, the family home houses Coupeville Yarns and the Whidbey Net offices.

So, when Ken Poteet thinned the tree, what happened to the maple? Bob Bailey, Marilyn's husband, is a farmer and a talented wood turner who, long ago, asked Wylie to call him if the maple tree were ever the cut.

Bob was called, and before Ken's saw started buzzing, the Bailey's trailer was in place at 202 N Main to load every usable fragment cut from the tree. The sections were taken to the Bailey home on Jacob's road and cut into slats in Bob's sawmill. It'll take a couple years for the pieces to dry enough to be usable, Marilyn said.

When the wood is ready, you can be sure Bob will create beautiful pieces, maybe even a bowl or two so Marilyn can have a bit of the maple tree of her childhood on her dining room table.

***

Why is it that the human suffering of those across the ocean is so much more important to us than the suffering of those on Whidbey Island?

***

I wasn't really sick, but I wasn't really not sick.....just kind of miserable. The TV was as miserable as I was until I switched over to Channel 9's *Sesame Street*. What fun! Even the commercials were great.

Have you seen that dog drink milk from a glass?

My disposition improved immediately. I recommend the music, the dance and the song to anyone who needs a little cheering up no matter how many candles graced your last birthday cake.

***

Our visit to Bandon was perfect....two days of sunshine and two of rain...the better to browse antique shops, my dear. No pressure, no time line. Wandered, poked, and made sure we didn't miss something that we had no idea we were looking for. Bought four (need five) Lusterware salad plates, but found no blue -- orange is not acceptable -- condiment sets.

Next time.

***

Maybe the overdue *Coupeville High School Connection* was in the back of my mind when I talked to Marilyn Bailey. However, it wasn't until she mentioned her mom that I realized I was talking to the daughter of one of the subscribers.

Then she reminded me that she is a 1948 CHS graduate, and also a subscriber, and that the newsletter is LATE.

I know that. I told her we *had* to go to Long Beach to baby-sit Gary's KayLynne and Emily, that we *had* to help my first grandchild Heidi Lynne plan her July wedding, that we *had* to go to Bandon, that we *have* to get ready for Sarah to come from Michigan to "interview" Western Washington State University.

Marilyn didn't give a hang about my whining. Even when I changed the subject to her great-granddaughter McKayla, Rusty's daughter, she was still talking about maybe she'd write a letter for the newsletter...since it was late.

So fine. I'll get the *CHS Connection* in the mail.

***

I'm so glad to be home again.

What's a 'couple' of bikes anyway? A big headache

June 27, 1997

No one knows better than Nic Hallett that both All Island Bicycles Rental and Rita's Rainbow Thrift & Gift Shop are actively doing business on North Main at 302 1/2.

Yes, the Nic Hallett who fills our prescriptions - - the Nic who is ready at a minutes notice to save our homes from flames — he's the Nic who also races around saving fair maidens in distress.

And he did it again Sunday morning.

The whole thing started when the ever growing Whidbey Net expanded into the area where building owner Peter Gnehm used to have his All Island Bicycles business. Peter moved all but a token bike or two into a less obvious part of his building and hired someone to take care of his customers.

It looked like the bike shop was no more.

Rita, whose shop is next door, offered to "rent out his bikes" for him. She also suggested it would help his business if he had a few bikes in view. So why not put a couple in front of her shop with a *for rent* sign?

Good idea...except for the little mix up.

A "couple" means different things to different people. And "For Rent" signs come in different sizes.

Sunday morning, Rita arrived at her shop to find many, many, many bikes parked across the front of her shop, a huge "For Rent" sign securely attached to her front window, and worse, a very excited gentlemen parked by her door waiting for someone to show up so he could rent the building.

"No, no, no!" Rita shooed him away. But she couldn't move the bikes and she couldn't reach the sign.

Enter Nic Hallett.

Actually, it wasn't that simple. Nic was all ready to race for the ferry when he received Rita's call for help. Given who Nic is, he HAD to rescue the lady. He arrived at her shop within minutes.

Rita said it was a sight to behold.

Nic drove up, left the motor running, leaped from his van with his screwdriver in his hand, his dog Haida at his heels, and in a flash, he had waded through the bikes to reach the "For Rent" sign, removed it from her window and he was out of there.

I had to ask... "was his van silver and was he wearing a mask?"

***

***

Al Sasso and his lady Marion, owners of The Victorian Bed and Breakfast, have a lot to be grateful for. Marion is home and recovering nicely after suffering a heart attack on June 7.

She says she should have known it was coming. In fact the night before, she experienced excruciating pain in her left arm, shoulder and hand and Al took her to Whidbey General ER where she was given an EKG.

As sometimes happens, the results were negative. A bad disc and/or her arthritis were blamed for the pain.

The next morning was a different story. "It felt like I had an elephant sitting on my chest," Marion said. "The pressure was unbearable."

A blood clot was diagnosed and "a clot buster was administered, expensive stuff," she says. "But it worked."

Marion was later taken off island where a successful angioplasty was performed.

This whole thing really "knocked them both for a loop."

The Sassos are a lot wiser today. They know they should have paid closer attention to the pain in Marion's left arm. They know she should have told her doctor about the "drawing" feeling she experienced in her jaw for so long. And that the chest pain people talk about isn't pain, it's a feeling of pressure — severe pressure.

A lot of things have changed. While in the hospital she says she told her doctor "not any more" when he asked her if she smoked. When he asked her when she quit, she said "right now."

Marion isn't taking any more chances. She's following doctors orders and paying attention to what her body is telling her, like stopping when she's tired. She is already walking around the block a couple times a day and staying on a strict diet.

That's her only gripe.

"If it tastes good," she laughs, "it's not good for me."

Marion will be OK.

***

Soroptimists do good things

July 4, 1997

If it's the first or third Tuesday of the month you've probably seen them going into Cam-Bey Apartments around noon.

They are a group of about 20 women of all ages and dress - - from designer suits to paint-splattered sweatshirts - - carrying sack lunches or those little Styrofoam boxes from the deli, all walking with confidence. The women are business owners, volunteers or they hold management positions in the community.

They are the Soroptomist International of Coupeville and they are listed on page 27 of MacGregor's Directory as an organization that "provides service to the local community through scholarships and grants." Well written given the 25 word limit, but a grossly understated description.

Soroptimists do provide scholarships to two graduating seniors each year, and through the Women Helping Women program, they assist with heat bills, rent, or perhaps a wardrobe for school, or work....whatever it takes to get the applicant on her feet.

And the Soroptomists provide a fund that teachers tap for students' emergency needs such as glasses, lunch money, or even money to rent musical instruments.

They also perform highway cleaup three times a year and work diligently with foreign exchange students.

The Soroptomists work hard and play hard.

When the members recognized that our community was being drained by so many organizations requesting donations, they assessed themselves and provided their own budget to donate for the grants and scholarships.

Beginning last January, they decided not to have fund raisers any more, they still raise money though, only it's called FUN raising.

It's a change of attitude. And it flows over into the social activities that sometimes include spouses, among them a Progressive Dinner, a Christmas Gold Dinner Dance, a Mystery Dinner, a Road Rally and a "Thrill at the Mill," a shopping trip to the Pendelton shop in Oregon.

The organization has received national recognition twice in their 10 years in Coupeville. The first was for the production of *In My Father's Bed*, a series of activities designed to help women who had been sexually abused by family members.

The second was for bringing Fevzijad and Nafija Hadzic, a young Bosnian couple, to the United States.

The International Goodwill and Understanding Committee (IGU) which included Jan Bronson, Julia Hodson, Ruby Dunn and the late Shirley Mayko knew the effort would be time consuming and intense as well as a financial strain but they were determined.

They knew that in Bosnia, Fevzijad had been an upscale business man who owned a successful photography studio. That during the war, everything was taken from them and that they had been living in a refugee camp in Turkey for 18 months.

When the couple arrived at Sea-Tac airport in early 1995, the committee went to work and the Whidbey Island community stepped forward.

The rental house the Soroptomists found for the couple was in need of repairs. A local contractor offered his services to make it "better."

A car was donated, the couple was given furniture, kitchen appliances, food and emotional support.

Language was a severe job barrier, Fevzijad had limited knowledge but Nafija could not speak a word of English. So Irene Carr, an English as a Second Language (ESL) teacher but not a Soroptomist member, volunteered her services. Irene taught the Hadzics English for the six months they were in Coupeville.

In mid 1995, the couple moved to St. Louis, Missouri to join the Bosnian community there. They have stayed in contact with several club members and report that just two years after arriving in the United States with nothing, the Hadzic's own a new car. Fevzijad is a long-distance truck driver in his own $50,000 semi truck, and Nafija works at the Embassy Suites. Truly an American dream come true. A story just right for the 4th of July.

The results of the actions of Soroptimist International of Coupeville, I'm told, "aren't splishy-splashy, but they are good things - - things that really make a difference in our community."

I agree. With everything they do - - provide scholarships, grants, emergency funds, cleaner roads, support for foreign students, or laughter and enjoyment, these 20-plus women improve our community.

If you would like to join them and engage in awareness, advocacy and action in the service of your community, call president Carol Bartelson 678-2259.

***

Happy 58th Wedding Anniversary,
Ethel and Palmer Kauffman!

Saving Sears house was community endeavor

July 11, 1997

It's like the old western movies.

You remember the plots? Settlers under siege fighting to save their water holes from the big, bad land barons. Families and neighbors standing shoulder to shoulder to protect their land. The children had sad little eyes and spoke words of wisdom that could break the strongest man.

The scenes always brought tears to the eye and pride to the heart when the good guys won.

The Greenbank community has been under siege for a long time.

There were plans for 700 houses to be built on Greenbank farm, then the state Department of Transportation and Island Transit wanted to build a park and ride at a beautiful lookout spot and turn it into a well-lit concrete nightmare. And, just this spring, DOT's demolition list included two of the island's oldest buildings, a house ordered through the Sears & Roebuck catalog at the turn of the century, the other, a repair shop older than most residents.

Each and everytime, families were right there standing shoulder to shoulder and their neighbors were with them.

And the good guys won. Everyone knew it wasn't just Greenbank in danger, it was a whole way of life.

The Berg fix-it shop and the little house by the side of the road still stand...uprooted and boarded shut...but still standing because of a worried little boy, hard work, and a stroke of luck.

Greenbank residents had seen so much of their community disappear during the widening of State Highway 525 - - mighty trees, beautiful hedges, anything in the way of the DOT's project. They were even ready to let the old shop go.

But when the pink flags surrounded the little white house on Greenbank farm, even 8-year-old Danny had had enough.

"They can't do that, mom, they can't just knock that down," he said. His mom, Sally Jacobson, agreed.

Sally called the president of Island County Historical Society, Joan Houchen, who hadn't been notified that the buildings were being destroyed. After some checking, Houchen said DOT officials told her both buildings had been examined by an expert and neither had any historical value. One had been altered and the other moved.

Joan knew moving and altering historical houses rarely changed their status, so Steve Emerson, Washington State Historian, was called for an opinion.

Emerson said the house could be registered if they could prove it was from Sears. Sears houses, he said, had numbers printed in the wood, sometimes in a door jam or in a window frame.

With two days until demolition, Sally and Randy Jacobson started looking. After a long search, they removed trim from one last door. They had to dislodge sheet rock probably installed in the early 1970s. Using a flashlight, they saw little bits of wallpaper with painted flowers in sparkly greens and a maroon colored tulip.

And they saw what looked like a brown paper bag covering the wall with a company name and the numbers SR2.

The Sears & Roebuck numbers.

Armed with verification from Sears, Houchen contacted the DOT. DOT said "OK." They'd even move both buildings for the historical society, but the location had to be decided by June 16 or work on the road would have to stop until spring.

That would leave Greenbank looking and feeling like a war zone.

Sites were found. The Berg shop is on the Jacobson property facing Day Road waiting to become a museum. Fitting.

The little Sears house was moved across the road onto the southwest corner of the farm where Coupeville port commissioner Lew Naddy says, "It can bask on it's own 1/2 acre forever."

The windows were boarded up for safety by four South Whidbey Rotarians, George Mackela, Ed Oetken, Robert Jimeniz and Joan Houchin. The house will stay boarded until renovation begins.

Once the house is on its foundation and the exterior painted, a story board will be erected telling about the house's history.

There may not be room to tell the rest of the story, including that the house was built to house farm workers and intentionally placed on the outskirts of the farm... as far as possible from the farmer's daughters.

Island County Historical Society has grand plans for the little house. Given the proper funds and an army of volunteers, the living room and the kitchen will be restored to their original condition. The two bedrooms, once holding bunk beds for workers, will be rented out as offices to groups that complement the activities of the farm.

Plans are firming up, right down to the landscaping. Master Gardener Don Lee has studied the area where the house once stood and listed the foliage there. The same plants will surround the new setting.

The historical society will maintain the buildings and grounds.

Good job. The good guys won!

Car accident puts life in perspective

July 18, 1997

When I left home Sunday morning, I was on my way to Southcenter to do a little shopping with my daughter before going to my granddaughter's wedding shower in Auburn.

In a blink of any eye, everything changed.

The lane I was in was moving so slowly I considered moving to either the left or right. Both lanes were running smoothly. Never had a chance. I was hit hard from behind and pushed forward so hard, I was barely able to stop before hitting the van ahead of me.

The young man who hit me was out of his car in an instant, as was I, to see what the heck happened. His hood was squished up by his windshield, the entire engine area was exposed and he was almost in tears.

It was a brand new car. What kind? Green.

Our Ford Ranger will never be the same. The bumper is still hanging on, but twisted under until the license plate is flat against the truck bed. Can't open the tailgate or it falls on the ground, and the whole back of the truck is cockeyed.

Inside, everything spilled everywhere. A cassette in the tape deck was dashed to the floor, the driver's seat won't sit up straight and the console is on a down hill roll. The truck was hauled off by a tow truck. I don't know why. For $159, I guess.

I was hauled off to Northwestern hospital on a board they called a stretcher. Held very, very still with a hard plastic neck brace and velcro straps fortified with what, I swear, was a huge role of duct tape. The strip across my forehead didn't help my raging headache. Spent over an hour on that board. One should be out cold when in that position. Then, x-rays and more x-rays. By that time, my Southcenter daughter and son Rick, who lives just around the corner from the accident, were at my side.

I was released with dire warnings about how I'd feel on Monday. They were right. It hurts if I move my neck or lift my arm. And yes, I went to Heidi's shower, but I went in jeans, with no gift and pretty shaky.

Rick picked up the truck and drove it home.

The point I want to make is that it happened in the blink of an eye. One minute I was sailing along, the next I was dead in the water. It could have been worse, it could have been all over.

We forget how precious life is and how quickly the world can change. Let's not forget again.

***

Just a year ago, on July 12, I wrote my first column for *The Coupeville Examiner*. It starred Lillian Huffstetler and the Shifty Sailors. We were so nervous and 53 columns later, we still get nervous.

Yes, it's a "we" thing. I make Gordie suffer too. But it's been awesome. I've met so many people, learned a lot. And I was right, every person has an important story to tell.

All we have to do is listen.

Thank you for your phone calls, your notes, your smiling faces and your words of encouragement. And more importantly, thank you for lettimg me write about you! It's been an amazing year.

***

Marilyn Libbey Bailey called about the June 20 column. She said her father, Joe W., had a sister, not a brother, named Jessie and he had another brother, Calvin. Calvin's widow, Anne, still lives in the Joseph Barstow Libbey house on North Main. Also, the house where Marilyn grew up, where WhidbeyNet, Coupeville Yarns and Rita's Rainbow Thrift & Gift all live now, is just a few paces from the Libbey house, not a "couple of blocks." Sorry, Marilyn.

***

This Sunday, July 20, I'll be a bit older and my whole family will be here to celebrate. Sunday is also Concerts on the Cove's first Sundays in the Park concert, a Scottish Festival. There will be dancing during the concert and a special beginners' session afterward.

Since my great-great-great-grandfather, Andrew McCornack, was born in Annabaglish, Wigtownshire, Scotland, it's high time we all learned how to do a Scottish dance or two.

How about you, can you come?

Shall we spend a couple hours together Sunday afternoon?

Let's do it.

See you at the Pavilion in Coupeville Town Park at 2 p.m..

Job swap a coup for the two Noras

July 25, 1997

More than once, when I'd see all those cars driving north to work "up here" while I was driving south to work "down there" at Boeing, I was tempted to jump out of my car, flag somebody down and say "Let's swap jobs! - - You take my job, I'll take yours!"

I'll bet you've had the same idea.

Well, two people on this island did exactly that. Nora Cashen and Nora Anderson, both physical therapy clerks at Whidbey General Hospital, made it happen.

Cashen lives in Coupeville. She's worked at WGH for nine years, seven of those years for critical care in Coupeville. In 1995, she switched to the physical therapy department, was hired by Whidbey General South in Clinton, and became part of the team that designed and operated the clinic.

She started riding the bus south to work every day and quickly found that she was in big trouble. Cashen has two children. At the time, her son Andrew was 12 and attended Coupeville Elementary School and her 10-year-old daughter Joivanna, a severe asthmatic, was being home schooled. If either one needed her in a hurry, the time it took for a transit bus to arrive was an eternity.

Anderson lived in Coupeville for 18 years. She had been working at WHG for six years when Whidbey General South opened in Clinton. A physical therapy clerk, she was offered the position at the South Clinic, but she said "no," she was just a hop from work right where she was - - she'd stay there.

Six months ago, things changed. Anderson sold her Coupeville house, built a beautiful home in Clinton, and started driving a long way to work.

So there they were. Every morning Cashen drove 20 miles south and Anderson drove 20 miles north. Each to their job as physical therapy clerks for Whidbey General Hospital.

The Noras waved at each other as they passed on highway 525, and they joked about living on the wrong end of the island but they didn't do anything about it until the snows came.

In December, the roads were bad, and the Clinton Nora struggled to get even as far north as the Whidbey General South to take the Coupeville Nora's place and the Coupeville Nora was grateful to fill in for the other Nora at WGH with a commute of only a few blocks from her home.

After the snows, the swapping jobs talk turned serious, an agreement was made, the boss said "yes," and on July 7, the trade was made.

Now, the south end Nora works in Clinton, and the north end Nora works in Coupeville.

The patients? Well, on the phone, the Noras answer for each other. They don't see any reason to explain the whole thing. But they do have to say something when a patient is standing in front of them frowning at the name tag and looking at the different face. So they tell them they wanted to keep it simple, and decided to use the same name.

That's about all that's the same.

Oh, and the humor. Both ladies are getting a tremendous kick out of the similarities. Think about it. How many Noras do you know? How many of them are physical therapy clerks? How many of them are employed by Whidbey General Hospital?

Both Noras love to tell the story of the "brilliant job swap." I have a feeling therapy patients have a better chance of a quick recovery with either one of them checking them in!

They are both delightful.

I still wonder if someone on Interstate 5 would have swapped jobs with me.

***

Because the metabolism slows down when a person quits smoking, the doctor says that a weight gain of 7-10 pounds is expected for a little while. But only 7-10. Any pounds over that amount are your pounds and have nothing to do with not smoking. OK! OK!

***

Get ready for another Concerts on the Cove's presentation.

This Sunday's performance, Strings of the Saratoga Chamber Players and SING!CHRONICITY, is in the Coupeville Elementary multipurpose room it starts at 2 p.m.

Whidbey Island's finest vocalists and musicians will entertain you for a couple hours.

What a neat way to spend a lazy Sunday afternoon.

'Painted places' judges tour by land, water

August 1, 1997

She had directed them into town past Fort Casey, thru Ebey's Prairie, and by the time they arrived at the Compass Rose B & B, they were hooked. Just as Rita Kuller had planned.

A Central Whidbey Chamber of Commerce member, Rita entered Coupeville in the "Prettiest Painted Places in America" contest by submitting 40 of the hundreds of pictures that photographer Judith Harper had taken at Rita's request.

And now, John Evans and John Stauffer of Rohm and Haas Paint Quality Institute (PQI), were here from Pennsylvania to check out the authenticity of those pictures.

Traveling that route, they were ready to believe.

Jan Bronson served coffee and muffins while we talked about PQI, the contest, and our guests. We knew Coupeville was one of five finalists in the northwest region in towns with less than 5,000 residents and would be judged in September by the PQI, *Architecture,* and *Better Homes and Gardens* magazines.

We knew we could win the contest and receive a commemorative plaque, highway signs announcing our distinction, and be the focus of a media campaign.

They told us PQI manufactures the raw ingredients that go into all brands of paint, so whenever paint is applied, they are interested. Perfection, they said, can be achieved by following four simple rules:

1. Take time to prepare the surface properly. 2. Buy only top quality paint. 3. Use high quality brushes and tools. 4. Paint under the right weather conditions.

They'll share more secrets on http://www.paintquality.com.

We learned that John Stauffer, director of PQI, was in the Peace Corps in the 1960s and today collects pool tables.

But that's another story.

Both Evans and Stauffer are experts on antique guns and found a match in Marshall Bronson, who knows every nook and cranny of Camp Casey, which guns were fired, which were stored where, and why.

Coffee finished, we went to check out the beautifully painted buildings that put us in the contest.

Rita drove Evans, PQI's public relation person, and Bronson drove John Stauffer. I went along and couldn't stop smiling...

It's always amazing to see how beautiful our world is through the eyes of a newcomer. We drove down Engle Road, to Fort Casey, to the beach, the cemetery, along Madrona, and into town. Actually, we didn't drive, we kind of started and stopped all along the way. Stauffer had his camera poised. Over and over, he grabbed the door handle. "Oh, I'd like one of that one too."

"Oh," he'd whisper, "If you could just pull over here."

Marshall stopped, and Stauffer took pictures of every house - - every view, sometimes walking long distances to get the perfect shot. By the second stop it was clear that 'painted places' had lost out to prairie magic. Stauffer took pictures of the block houses, the light house and what he called "super barns." He also shot the homes of Lois McGinnes and Marguerite Walker.

"Just let me hop out," he'd say, and he'd snap a dozen shots of the Colonel Crockett B&B, the water, the prairie, the house on Cathedral Drive...he was enchanted. And when his camera's battery grew weak, Bronson went to Coupeville Pharmacy for a new one.

In the meantime, Rita was driving John Evans around town with his video camera. She called Frank Pustka, of Whidbey Water Works, mentioned the contest, and asked if he could take Evans out to get some shots from the water side. "Did Frank have time?"

Rita said he didn't miss a beat. "When can you be here?" Frank was ready. He'd "do whatever it took...I want Coupeville to win."

Evans had never seen such a sight. "We were in luck," Frank said. "The good Lord blessed us with water as flat as a pancake and with people waving from the dock - - it was perfect."

As was the day.

The gentlemen from the Rohm and Haas Paint Quality Institute left to check out LaConner later than planned - - a bit rushed and a bit dazed with all they'd seen. Coupeville showed well and it would be wonderful to win the *Prettiest Painted Places in America* contest. However, we are surrounded by beautiful homes, beautiful businesses, beautiful scenery, beautiful people.

We're already winners.

***

Concerts on the Cove presents an exceptional group this Sunday in the park. Called ASZA, they bring us the Music of the World. Nominated for Canada's Juno Award, the four musicians, two from Canada, one from China and one from Uruguay, play a variety of exotic instruments to entertain us. 2 p.m. Aug. 3 in the pavilion.

***

Happy Anniversary,
Lori and Jack Miller & Mary Beth and Ken Adair.

Little flower girls had their own agenda

August 8, 1997

Saturday, July 26, in a magnificent outdoor ceremony at Three Tree Point in Seattle, our beautiful granddaughter Heidi and Stephen, her gallant prince, became one.

Every detail was perfect. Every detail.

Well, the littlest flower girls did have a different agenda. There were three in all, the maid of honor's daughter Tori, 4, who knew why she was at the wedding, and granddaughter KayLynne and great-granddaughter Amanda, both 2 who didn't.

All three paraded daintily down the staircase exactly as practiced, in step and smiling. However, the moment the 2-year-olds were in place in front of everyone, they started removing the flowers from their bouquet holder one by one. They each had about half a bouquet left when the soloist started singing sweet loving words and, as if on cue, they both sat down.

Then it was serious "rip that flower out" time. The girls were really into yanking every blossom out of their holders and dashing each one to the floor. Before the song was over, they had dismantled their bouquets completely.

I don't know what happened. The music was peaceful, everyone was smiling (broader & broader), Puget Sound was calm and our Mt. Rainier was beautiful.

The girls were oblivious to it all and to us. When it was time for the wedding party to move out, they knew exactly what to do.

KayLynne and Amanda stood up, smoothed their dresses, straightened their little shoulders and followed the happy couple down the aisle smiling all the way...bouquet holders firmly in hand, but not one flower between them.

***

Jenny spent Sunday with us, so we did some of the best of Coupeville. After church we enjoyed Tyee's brunch, Concerts on the Cove's presentation of ASZA in Town Park, Toby's hamburgers, and a spin around Penn Cove on the Whidbey Water Works party barge. What a kick floating about on a roomy pontoon.

We'll do that again.

***

During the concert intermission, the ASZA musicians answered our questions about the instruments they've gathered from all over the world. We learned the names and were able to hold some of the fascinating pieces for a bit.

Randy Raine-Reusch, a Canadian born composer who owns a personal collection of 500 exotic instruments, half jokingly told how he learned to play so many of them.

"I'm convinced I have Attention Deficient Syndrome," Raine-Reusch said, "As soon as I learned to play an instrument, I lost interest and went on to learn a new one. I'm ready to learn another one anytime."

***

I used to sew. Easy, just measure, cut, hem.

No more. I was afraid to cut one snip so I called Caroline King, who recognizes panic. She assured me that all would be OK and she could and would solve my problem.

She is a life saver. Caroline is still recovering from a broken wrist and dislocated left hand sustained in a fall over a year ago which led to surgery on her shoulder. She still has a long way to go before she's back stitching up beautiful things on a regular basis.

King says she has stacks of jobs to finish, but can only spend about 10 minutes at a time on any one movement...some activities she can do for an hour, but that's rare. Her muscles are not ready yet. "We take so much for granted," Caroline said, "I was thrilled when I could finally squeeze the tube of toothpaste !"

Do hang onto her phone number, Caroline will be back!

Thanks, lady.

***

A big weekend coming up! The Arts & Crafts Festival is a time of music, admiring and buying and selling beautiful creations, eating great food and renewing old friendships.

At Meerkerk Rhododendron Gardens, from 1-5 p.m.on Saturday, the first of three Whidbey Island Folk Festivals. Kristi O'Donnell says this concert has, for a small fee, three one-hour sets featuring fine artists.

You can do both festivals, no problem. Relax, wind down, bring a quilt and picnic on the lawn. You deserve it.

***

One month from today, September 8, we land at Heathrow Airport to spend three weeks tracing our roots and chasing dreams in England, Scotland and Ireland. Yes! Bill Bradkin at Coupeville Travel is setting us up for there, and for here, the line is long with offers to house sit.

It's old home week for Gookins clan

August 15, 1997

The Gookins family found last week that you CAN go home again. As they've done many times before, about 100 family members met Saturday at Fort Casey, to picnic, laugh together, share memories, and catch up on what's new.

Gordon Gookins calls it the "Gookins' Family Rebellion."

"We're a very close family, we love each other half to death and would do anything in the world for each other," he said.

He rented Frank and Reni Pustka's vacation house for his sister Bessie for the weekend. But the vacation house is more than that. It's the Captain Thomas Kinney house, where the Gookins kids grew up. Gordon couldn't wait to see Bessie's face when she realized where she was staying. Bessie's San Diego son Rick, his wife Alice, and sons Matt and Darren would stay there too, Gordon told Reni, and they'd arrive at about 3:30 in the afternoon.

What Gordon didn't know was that Reni had a surprise for him too - - a huge banner plastered across the front of the Kinney house which read "Welcome Home Gordon, Bessie & Leone!"

Right on time, the cars started arriving. Then Gordon drove up. He stepped out of his car, saw the sign, and he should have seen the look on *his* face! Coming home is always an emotional time, but that welcome sign did him in.

Gordon says it couldn't have been better. He and his sisters went through every inch of the house together sharing memories. They talked about the huge kitchen table that he could barely peek over as a child. "For a long time, my view of the world was the underside of that table."

They talked about playing marbles in the house and how the floors sloped downhill. Any marbles lost during a game would eventually roll to one corner of the dining room. They talked about the big rock on the beach in front of the house. The rock's indentation held colored glass and shells when the tide went out, and Gordon loved to play with them. It was his very own "secret place." Now, he knows it was everyone's "secret place."

There was a toy dump truck in the mercantile store (now the Antique Mall) on Front Street. Gordon wanted that truck with all his heart and remembers exactly where it was in the store. He still wishes he had it. That's one of the lessons of his life. He says if someone had bought it for him, it probably would have broken and he would have forgotten about it. Instead, 60 years later, he still remembers that truck. Sometimes wishing is better than having.

Saturday, the talk and the memories went on and on and the yard was full of kids having a great time. Just like he remembered. Sunday, it started all over again.

The Gookins family bought the Kinney house in 1920, when Gordon's dad, William F. Gookin, was Island County Sheriff. Gordon, the youngest, was born there four years later. When he was 13, the family moved off the island.

He's returned many times to visit and to check out the old house, however. That's how he met the Pustkas. Gordon has painted every house he's ever owned yellow and white, so when he saw his old Coupeville home being painted the "right colors," he had to stop. "When I told them (the Putskas) who I was, they wanted to know all about the house." It's close to what it was and yes, the floors are finished - - but they still slope.

Tuesday mornings, Gordon volunteers at the Island County Museum where he met Ethylee Maylor. He says he couldn't believe it when Ethylee knew his family. She knew them all: Alice, Leone and Bessie and the two boys, Bill and Gordon.

Alice and Herb Allwine raised seven children at Fort Casey; Leone and Bill Christie raised three in Bellingham. Since 1939, Bessie has lived in Arizona, where she and Jack Housand raised five children. Luella, Bill's wife, still lives in Mount Vernon and has two sons.

Gordon has one daughter, and he and his wife Leslie live south of Greenbank. Sometimes they wish they had settled in Coupeville. "But," Leslie says, "maybe the town's magic will last longer if we just visit now and then."

Gordon has wonderful stories to tell about when his dad was sheriff and when he wasn't, about how his dad ran the bar and the card room in the Central Hotel until it burned down, how the bar he brought from the fort ended up at Toby's Tavern. Read the inscription. He'll tell you about his mom Katie, who worked to support the family. He'll also tell you how his older sisters and brother "kinda raised me with their children," so his nieces and nephews are more like brothers and sisters.

When the old Conard house was moved in behind the Kinney house, lilac bushes that his mother had planted in 1920 had to be removed. "Soon as I saw that, I borrowed a pickup and brought two of them home. They're planted in my back yard where they belong."

"I have nothing but good memories of the old house," he said. "We were poor when I was growing up, but I didn't know it. As far as I knew, I was the richest kid in the world."

Gordon Gookins still is.

Pull up a haystack and enjoy the wedding

August 22, 1997

Sunflowers in gunny sack vases, bales of straw, western attire, and a barbecue. Doesn't sound like a wedding, does it? Well it is!

On Saturday, August 23, Dean Staples of Windsor, Virginia, and Mary Taylor, daughter of Ellie and Lynn Taylor of Coupeville, will marry at her parents' home on Calhoun Loop in Admirals Cove. Mary's children, Michael Taylor, 7, and Taylor Lynn, 4, will hold places of honor, as will Jeremy Lee, Dean's eight-year-old son who will be ring bearer.

This whole thing happened pretty fast.

Mary was living in Virginia when she met Dean. They decided this was *IT* and Mary called her mom. "We want to get married August 23." That was five weeks ago. Ellie told her that was pretty short notice, was Mary sure she wanted to move that fast?

Mary was indeed sure and she was willing to accept whatever her mom decided for their wedding. So, Ellie told her "fine, with only five weeks, I am going to tell you what to do, and you are going to do it - - exactly." Mary accepted, as in "Yes, Mommy, you've never made a decision for me that I didn't like!"

So it's done. Everything was ready when Mary came home a couple of days ago. The wedding hat is beautifully draped in lace, netting, and flowing ribbons, and the bouquets are arranged. The cake is ready and topped with a bride and groom dressed in western attire all soft and frilly with blue lace.

The patio has dozens of stacked straw bales for seating and there are sunflower bouquets and baskets of flowers everywhere... and music.

Music to listen to, cry to, and dance to.

None of this "a reception will follow the ceremony" stuff, Ellie said. "It's a barbecue, we're serving down-home cooking....potato salad, baked beans, smoked salmon, roast turkey and, besides the cake, my special dessert."

Mary's friends and family, her aunt Annie and her mom have planned the wedding by phone, at home, and while Annie created beautiful nails and Ellie performed miracles with her scissors at the Genesis Hair & Tanning in Coupeville.

They've sent no formal invitations. "The family's been here forever, and we don't want to forget to invite anyone," Ellie said. "We want all of our friends to come join with us to celebrate Mary and Dean's wedding."

When you go to the wedding, hug them for you, then hug them for me, especially the kids, Michael Taylor, Taylor Lynn and Jeremy Lee.

Love is a splendid thing, share it.

***

Dorothea Jones had a twinkle in her eyes the day she told me she'd given up cooking for the summer. KC nodded in agreement.

She told me she wasn't as involved in community work as when we served on the chamber's HarvestFest committee together. Twice, she took applications for craft booths and made sure all went well with the artists in the multipurpose room. In 1992, she worked as part of a committee of Whidbey Pride Lions, but the next year, she just did it by herself.

Then she quit. She said she'd served her time. Of course, she was only 87 then and had other things to do.

She enjoys a little gardening now and then, and is busy going out to dinner "and stuff" with KC. They've been married for 62 years. In fact, Dorothea says, she can't remember when she wasn't married.

They led a busy life in Pasco where she started teaching high school English before she was married and taught for 30 years, and KC worked for the Bonneville Power Authority.

Dorothea and KC moved to Coupeville from Pasco in 1976, but Dorothea knew all about Whidbey long before that. Actually, more than 60 years ago, her roommate brought Dorothea here to visit her cousin, Dorothy Sherman. That was before there was a bridge over Deception Pass and, Dorothea says, before there was an Al Sherman.

Al told me that yes, he knew Dorothea and his mother were friends for many, many years. And, he said, he knows that Dorothea Jones is a very special kind of person who cares about others and does something about it.

Dorothea, he said, was the one in the United Methodist Women's organization who saw to it that Phim and Phouvieng Khongsa were brought to Coupeville.

Carmen McFayden told me the same things about the lady.

Dorothea just brushes off "all that talk."

At 92, Dorothea had her second cataract surgery a couple weeks ago and admits to a long-ago knee replacement, but, she said, all the bits and pieces are working fine!

"Now you know," she said with a laugh, "it's got to be because of my good, pure living!"

I'm a believer, Dorothea, just keep it up!

Fragile poppies thrive under Wilbur's care

August 29, 1997

Wilbur Jennings loves the Mexican Matilija poppy, railroads, hats, kids, antique glass, and, most of all, his wife Maxine.

Because they married late in life, Maxine and Wilbur celebrate their wedding anniversary on the 16th of every month. Maxine tells me they just celebrated their 100th.

"She does the housekeeping, I do the cooking, and," Wilbur said, "we share the garden. I do the vegetables, she does the flowers." Except for the Matilija poppies. Those belong to Wilbur.

He's been raising the beautiful white poppy for 40 years, ever since his sister-in-law bought three plants in Seattle and gave one to each of her daughters and one to Wilbur.

His plant was the only one that survived. Over the years, he's given plant starts to dozens of expert gardeners but not one could keep them alive. He's not surprised. "Even my plants didn't do too well this year, they were only 6 feet tall. Normally," he chuckled, "they're closer to nine."

Wilbur knows all about the Mexican Matilija. "It grows wild as far north as the San Diego high desert, and receives attention much like our rhododendrons - - with tours and coverage in *Sunset* Magazine."

In 1949, the flower was on the cover of the magazine with a three-page spread about the many dollars spent on tests trying to start Matilija's from seed. No test was successful. That was 50 years ago and today's *Sunset* "Western Garden Book" still doesn't offer much hope. "You can try with seeds...and hope for sprouting."

Maybe Wilbur could show them how. He has them blooming on both of the properties he and Maxine own.

And he's watched the process. A couple of years ago, he decided it was time he saw it happen. He knew the poppies open during the night, and he could recognize which buds would be beautiful blooms by morning. He knew they had to be the size of his thumbnail and have a sliver of white showing through.

He chose two buds and took them into his house. Then he set the alarm for one hour and started playing solitaire. For nine hours, Wilbur played solitaire, and every hour when the alarm rang, he took a picture of the two buds and set the alarm again.

At exactly 6 a.m., the flower opened.

The Matilija poppy is six inches wide and has a 2-inch center of brilliant gold. The six petals of the flower look and feel like crepe paper and smell wonderful.

"It was well worth the wait."

The photographs are a panorama of splendor.

Wilber's other loves?

The Jennings were one of the original families in Marysville. After his parents died, he and his siblings donated the family's 12.5 acres to the city for the *Jennings Memorial Park*. Wilbur's eyes sparkle when he talks about the park's ball diamond and the fishing pond for kids under 14.

Then there's his hat collection.

One hundred and fifty hats hang neatly on both sides of the beam in the living room. He says he probably bought 50 of the hats, the rest came from family and friends. He believes he is the owner of a hat unique to employees of Bayliner's New Orleans factory. His grandson arranged for that one for him.

Wilbur won his railroad hat in a raffle in Skykomish. But he had already earned the right to wear it. He was a locomotive engineer for the railroad for 30 years working out of Seattle.

"In those days, we had to work as a fireman for three years before we advanced to engineer."

"Today," he said, "they give college kids a three-week course and they're in."

When he started, it was called the Great Northern Railroad. In 1970, with a merger, it became the Burlington Northern.

He retired on July 3, 1974 with great memories and mementos.

In 1962, he rescued five pieces of stained glass in lead settings from an 1863 Great Northern Coach car headed for the scrap pile. Today, they are beautifully mounted on his dining room wall.

On his mantel, he has an original switchman's lantern, used for flagging, and a framed check for 24 cents from the Great Northern Railroad dated February 28, 1948.

The check is made out to him, but was signed and cashed by another railroad man. Wilbur will have to tell you about that.

And, I bet, he'll tell you more about the Mexican Matilija poppy too.

It's right up there on the top of his list of loves.

Just below Maxine.

Texas transplant finds island picture perfect

September 5, 1997

After living in Texas for 25 years, Judith Harper toured the United States with a favorite aunt and, by the time they reached Bellingham, she was in love with the Northwest.

She knew she had to live here, but Bellingham didn't feel like "home" nor did Anacortes or LaConner.

A trip to Deception Pass changed her life. When the first person she saw smiled and greeted her, Judy jumped on it. "Where are you from?" she asked.

The lady was from Whidbey Island, and Judy was hooked. She moved to Coupeville, and she's not leaving.

For a year, she's been living in an apartment on Front Street, keeping an eye on Penn Cove and Mt. Baker. "I've enjoyed the sunrise every single morning, and in a few days, I'll be in my own home enjoying the sunsets."

"I love this island," she said, "and I'm thrilled to be in Coupeville. Everyone and everything is so dynamic. There is so much community action!"

Judy's already into community action. When Rita Kuller learned she only had two days to enter Coupeville in the *Prettiest Painted Places in America* contest, she asked local artisans for a list of the best photographers. She needed someone who could take great pictures of Coupeville without aggravating anyone. And she needed that person to do it for nothing.

Bottom line: An expert, tactful, and diplomatic photographer willing to work for naught for the good of the entire community was needed. Judith Harper was on that list, and she said she'd do it, she'd take the pictures.

And she did it well. Forty of the dozens of pictures she took were submitted. Because of those photos, Coupeville is in the running.

Funny thing about Judith Harper. Before moving to Coupeville, she was pretty much a people photographer. Now, more and more of her time is spent taking shots of the breathtaking scenery and catching the constantly changing light.

But she still paints. Her superb creations are on display in offices all over Houston, Texas and Portland, Oregon, and now they can be seen at the Penn Cove Gallery and Old Town Shop on Front Street.

Monday, Judith spent a couple hours patiently explaining her painting techniques to this person, who doesn't have an artistic bone in her body. She talked one-of-a-kind, ghost images, atmosphere, print making and plexiglas until she realized I wasn't getting any of it. So she promised to give me some hands-on another time and dropped it.

Then her eyes lit up and she brought out the 1997 *Arnazella Arts* magazine, published by Bellevue Community College and opened it to *her* page. "I'm a published poet," she said with delight. "I am a recognized painter and photographer, but to have my words in print, that's the best!"

Nothing pleases her more. Besides a soul-searching poem about fear, three of her photographs are included in the publication. She says most of her poetry is light and funny and that's what she'll submit for her next entry. And there will be a next one.

Other than that, Judith does some yoga and loves every kind of dance, including contact improvisation. We do that naturally, she said. As we move about expressing ourselves, we are "doing our dance. It's what we need to do when we're in front of a camera. We need to let our body take charge. Your body knows what to do."

"Let it go, be yourself and your picture will be great," she advised.

We're going to see a lot more of Judith Harper, painter, photographer, poet and community person. Count on it!

***

Mike Sullivan is finding it a little difficult to get around on his own two feet after wearing a cast on his right foot for weeks and weeks. Now that it's over, ask him how he drove his vehicle.

***

Time has run out to do all of the things we had planned for "later this summer," for all the projects, the time we planned to spend with our grandkids, for preparing for our trip to England, Scotland and Ireland.

It's over. We have to be packed and out of here Monday morning. Are we ready? Nope, but we're going anyway.

Janet Enzmann, Jane Jones, Emily Hancock, Jim and Joyce Cavanaugh, to name just a few, had wisdom to share on what to do and what not to do on the trip. I was going to check them out "later." But "later" is here, and some I did, some I didn't. Doesn't matter, the trip is going to be magnificent.

Our housesitter is ready to jump on the ferry, Melissa the cat has orders to behave and, in a minute I'm turning off my computer.

Talk to you later!

Co-op preschool still has openings for students

September 12, 1997

Parents, there are still openings at the Central Whidbey Cooperative Preschool in Coupeville. Dig out your March 7, 1997 edition of *The Examiner* and learn about the activities you and your child could be enjoying.

Or call Cindy at 678-6782.

***

If everything has gone as planned, we picked up our car in Glasgow, Scotland this morning, and tomorrow we celebrate our 17th anniversary in Newton Stewart, Wigtownshire. Exactly where my great-great-great-grandfather was born!!

***

Because of the rain and wind, the last presentation of Concerts on the Cove's 1997 Sundays in the Park series was held in the multipurpose room at Coupeville Elementary School.

It didn't matter.

The North Cascade Concert Band, directed by Dr. Keith Eide, belted out Souza marches to a cheering and clapping full house and Piper Eger and Chad Summervill received standing ovations for raising goose bumps on 99 percent of those present with their *Phantom of the Opera* offerings.

It was a dazzling finale of yet another successful season.

Concerts on the Cove has been having successful seasons for many years. That's why I was surprised when a long-time resident asked "who and/or what is 'concerts'?"

I've been looking for a reason to tell you!

Concerts on the Cove is a nonprofit organization guided by a volunteer board of directors with a membership that probably includes, if not you, certainly more than a few of your neighbors.

Since it was formed in 1987, COC has been dedicated to bringing the finest in performing arts to Whidbey Island and has firmly established itself as a major contributor to the enrichment of the cultural life of our community.

Now you know who or what COC is and what we do.

Now let me tell you how it happens. The first Wednesday of every month at 7 p.m., a hearing room in the courthouse comes alive with ideas and discussions. Members of COC's board of directors discuss, discard, reshape and discuss again the how to's of accomplishing their goal: to bring to you the most talented artists available and to present those artists in the best possible way.

COC board members are hard working, fun, strong willed, intelligent, and extremely verbal. Most members attend every meeting even though they are very busy people. Every member has a job. Every member does their job. And more. Oh, there have been mistakes. Bad, bad, bad mistakes. But we've only made each one once.

In 1992, Concerts on the Cove built the pavilion in Town Park, and the grand structure was donated to the town of Coupeville. For five weeks every summer, that pavilion takes on a life of it's own.

Each Sunday afternoon, a different kind of music can be heard: maybe the stirring beat of the Air Force Concert Band, the vibrant rhythm of Laura Love, or the soothing strings of the Saratoga Chamber Players.

Island residents and travelers from as far away as Portland and Vancouver, British Columbia bring their lawn chairs and clap and cheer and sometimes, go down front to dance to the beat.

Best of all, Town Park is just that, a park with swings and a place for kids to run where they don't disturb the audience, but where they can hear the music.

Ergo: the enrichment of the lives of our youth.

The *Sundays in the Park* series has become very important to our community, as have the special presentations of music, drama, and dance gathered by COC from all over the world, among them the great Vladimir Russian Chorus, a SingAlong Messiah, the California based All American Boys Chorus and, this past spring, the Chilean Pozo Almonte choir with the Seattle Peace Chorus.

Often, artists offer special concerts for Coupeville students and when Shakespeare's *Taming of the Shrew* and *Twelfth Night* were presented, the board made sure workshops were included for the kids. For several years, talented young people were awarded scholarships through the COC sponsored Youth Showcase.

Friday, October 24 our first fall event brings the leading British a cappella trio, Artisan, appearing in the Performing Arts Center in Coupeville. They are magnificent. Don't miss them!

No matter how hard any group works, without community involvement and commitment, they can't succeed.

Concerts on the Cove is very fortunate.

Dozens of you support us in as many ways. Young Bryce and Matt Seltveit's support has already started. The two were pressed into service at the last concert to run for programs and cookies. We believe the enrichment of the lives of our youth takes many forms.

You are invited to be a part of one great group of people.

On the road in the United Kingdom

September 19, 1997

Good morning from Dublin, Ireland!

Just walked down the cobble streets of Dublin on Fleet Street to the Temple Bar area to use this computer in front of me. Cyber cafes are hard to come by around here.

What a time we've already had.

Day 1

Stayed in the Central Park Hotel right across from Hyde Park.

The number of people still bringing flowers and silently standing in line to sign the condolence book for Princess Diana is amazing.

They are a people in mourning.

Walked down Queensway street. No one spoke English, nor could we find an English restaurant.

The energy of the people walking around is electrifying.

We finally settled on a German restaurant mainly because diners were singing wonderful German songs.

When we were seated inside, though, all we could hear was a violinist playing American show tunes and *Take Me Out to the Ballgame.*

Day 2

Walked through Hyde Park on the way to the Marble Arches area to catch the double decker tour bus. People poured off the subway, called the "tube" here, arms full of flowers for the Princess.

Silent.

The park is well cared for, with people strolling about. Very civilized. Canvas sling chairs are set out early each morning, about 200-300 of them. They rent for 70 pence per day. No dogs, no children. Just quiet.

There are monuments everywhere and statues on buildings. So much to see, too much to see, in fact.

Got off the bus in Piccadilly Circus had a Guinness and fish & chips. Talked to some fellows from Birmingham, who were attending the World Cup Soccer playoffs. The place was loaded with fans from all over.

Then, to Westminster Abbey. The front lawn is full of flowers and tributes to Diana and her young princes.

There are always tears.

We went inside the abbey and were able to attend the 5 p.m. service. We sat in the seats the choir sat in during the funeral.

To be sitting there. I cried.

Day 3

Took the train to Glasgow, Scotland. The countryside is green and lush and swarming with sheep. Fences are stone or neatly trimmed hedges winding every which way, sometimes to keep cows and sheep apart, sometimes just to be.

The houses are stone or brick. I can hardly breath for the beauty. Arrived in the rain and were sent out on a five minute walk to our hotel. Never believe the British about their "five minute walks." They are much, much longer most of the time.

Walked to George square. Again, two complete areas piled high with flowers. While we are here, the parks department removed the flowers two or three bunches at a time. Almost reverently.

The messages will be kept, the good flowers sent to hospitals.

George Square has huge monuments, including an 80-foot memorial to poet Robert Burns. The Scottish people love Burns and, if they can, claim he spent time in their town.

Day 4

Took the grand tour.

Glasgow is just emerging as a tourist town. Still wears the scars and grime of its industrial period. Sadly, in the middle of town on four opposite corners, in buildings hundreds of years old, are McDonalds, KFC, Pizza hut, Dunkin' donuts.

But this is where we began our greatest adventure. We rented a car and Gordie drove - - on the left side of the road.

It was hair-raising - - to say the least. He did very well and only panicked a couple times. Hardest time was when cars came at him over a hill and he started to pull to the right to avoid them. He would remember, just in time, that everyone was right where they belonged.

I've lost a day in my report, but it doesn't seem to matter. My time on this machine is up. Just know that we are having the time of our lives.

Last night, Sept. 16, we went to The Harp, a pub in Sword just out of Dublin. The music was live. An accordion, snare drums and a mandolin. The drummer had a voice to die for and the group played for hours the songs my dad sang, as well as American show tunes. They love them and know every single word. Gordie thought he had died and gone to heaven. I knew I had. The whole pub made us welcome. It was a dream come true.

I may not get back to you, so, yes, I have stood in the house my great- great-great-grandfather was born in and the church he and his wife were married in. I may never survive.

Talk to you later.

It really IS a long way to Tipperary

September 26, 1997

Good morning from Galway!

It's getting harder and harder to remember what day it is, where we've been, or where we have to go next.

We were wise enough to leave our schedule loose, but we still have to be in London to catch our flight on Monday.

Every time we stop it's hard to get going again. Each place is so charming, the people so friendly, we could stay forever.

I can't tell you any more about our days in Scotland when I have to keep my eye on the clock. It was too precious a time. Maybe after we get home.

In Tramore, out of Waterford, we found our hostess, Marie Murphy, to be so gracious, we stayed a second night. She sent us to the O'Shea Hotel for dinner and music.

The Irish prepare salmon to perfection, their service is charming, and the music divine. You can't go wrong.

Water and ice are very hard to come by but when we insist, they appear. Gordie is always asked to repeat his request for ice cubes for his coffee. Some waitresses just raise their eyebrows and 'humor' him, but most can't help but laugh out loud. Shannon and Becky at Coupeville's Tyee have spoiled him completely.

The music, the music. In the O'Shea pub we found John O'Conner, who knows every American show tune and every Irish song ever written, including *I'll Take You Home Again, Kathleen.* Bought his tape, swapped snail and e-mail addresses, invited him to come sing in our town, and said good-bye like old friends.

Next morning we toured the Waterford Crystal Factory. Watched the entire process, from glass blowing to engraving. The outside of the pieces are much smoother than Gordie remembered his mother's pieces being. We were told the process is a bit different and, if he owned those sharper pieces, they would be worth a fortune.

Unfortunately, he doesn't.

Had lunch on the way to see the Rock of Cashel in County Tipperary. Ordered a potato topped with ham and cheese, but our plates came loaded. The potato came with potato salad, coleslaw, sliced tomatoes and cucumber and sliced eggs under mayonnaise with chopped onions over all. Must be more careful what we order, so much more arrives. Worse, we have to eat it all because it's so good.

The Rock of Cashel, the remains of a royal fortress and chapels, dates back 16 centuries. Our guide told us many tales, including St. Patrick's baptism of King Aengus. During the ceremony, by error, St. Pat drove the point of his staff through the King's foot. Thinking it was a public test of his faith, the king said nothing. However, the dozens of converts who were waiting their turn to be baptized fled to avoid the same test.

At Annette's B&B, yesterday, our 15th day here, we had breakfast served just the way I'd hoped it would be

All other B&B's have served us at separate tables with everyone's back to each other. We came here to meet people and to laugh together. Annette's had a large oval table with three couples visiting and sharing not only our current plans, but telling about home and family.

Both couples were from England and, at my request, they taught me how to eat European style. The main rule is to never, never, never, while eating European, turn the fork over to scoop in the food.

Oops, are we scoopers?

Today we go to Monaghan, where both sides of my family lived 100 years apart in time. Then, it's on to Poyntz Pass to chase a clue that Gordie's grandmother attended school there at the age of 10.

We'll spend a couple days in Dublin, return to England and then, home.

We've driven to Tipperary, and let me assure you, it is a long, long way.

We've attended an Irish wedding in Cobh, a wedding dance in Killarney, we've crossed the River Shannon, and visited the Cliffs of Moher.

It was while at the cliffs that I forgot, once again, that what goes up, must come down. Heights frighten me just a wee bit less than water, but excitement often clouds my judgment.

To see the cliffs more clearly, they say, one should climb the lookout tower. Many, many, many steps up a steel spiral staircase.

Up we went and down we came. Very, very, very slowly.

Gordie walked ahead and talked me back to earth.

The view from the ground was equally as clear. Like every view in Ireland, it doesn't get any better.

***

Kind people make up for pay phones, toilets

October 3, 1997

In Cobh, County Cork, there is a statue of the first Irish woman to enter Ellis Island.

Only 16, she is shown with her younger brother and sister as they leave Ireland for America. Their grief is obvious. I thought of them many times as we traveled their beautiful country and met the descendants of those they left behind.

I began to understand a wee bit.

We saw the reason for their grief in Monaghan, where they made time for us when we arrived - - unannounced - - at the Office of Ancestry. History books, church and legal records were searched in vain for our Monaghan roots. Local records don't go back to the 1700s. We were given addresses and thanked for coming!

We saw it again when I was calling B&B's. The phones were driving us mad. There are two systems. With one, the coins are deposited before dialing, and with the other, coins are deposited when the party answers.

For whatever reason, the called person doesn't seem to know it takes a moment to deposit coins, so they hang up and must be dialed again. Worse, both systems are timed. When the time is up, the call is over...NOW.

Sleeping in the car began to sound fine one evening, when Emily, a lovely Irish lass took over. She dialed, told them it was "Aunty Emm," said we needed a place to stay and that she was bringing us right out. She led us to the door, saw us in and drove off.

On a bus, the driver was having a bad day and was very rude. Before leaving the bus at their stops, every passenger walked back to give us the information we had asked the driver for.

All rest rooms are spotless, and most require advance payment - - some even have turnstiles, and prices, of course, differ. Twice, as I struggled to get the right amount of pence, someone just dropped the coins in and smiled me through.

In Northern Ireland, while we waited for the sexton in a charming little house "across the bridge," the finest china, silver and linen napkins were set and we were served tea and dainty sandwiches and wonderful Irish stories - - just because.

I understood how hard it would be to leave the kindness. Forever.

I didn't want to go across the border, but when we learned at Armagh that the Castle where Gordie's grandmother spent her childhood was near Poyntz Pass, we were on our way.

Yes, we were in Armagh and in Markethill, where a 400 pound bomb in a van exploded that week. Yes, soldiers with raised guns were in Poyntz Pass and at the border. Last week I said heights and water were my greatest fears. Add guns to the list.

The rest of the trip was delightful, except for one B&B. The favorite? Maybe in Skerries on the Irish Sea where the waves pounded on the rocks all night and where we climbed on those rocks before breakfast.

Maybe in Swords. A neat little town where moms push their babies in buggies or strollers like they do all over Ireland, shopkeepers remembered us, and where our favorite pubs were in full swing.

By the way, Irish pubs are not like our bars. Whole families have dinner in pubs, and then the kids play together inside and in the parking lot until 6:30 p.m. - - the signs say - - and neighbors and friends socialize. Later, the singing gets louder and the dancing a bit faster, but no one is out of control.

It was almost time to go home, and we were scheduled to take the ferry back to Holyhead on Saturday, catch the train into London, find a bed for a couple of nights, then ride the tube to Heathrow in time to catch our flight. The more exhausted we became, the longer and more difficult the return trip sounded. So we bought airline tickets from Dublin to Heathrow to home. We haven't discussed the cost. Whatever it was, the price was right. With two more days in Ireland, we relaxed.

Went into Dublin to do the tour but traffic was so bad we got off the bus at Trinity College, saw the Book of Kells then we walked - - yes, walked - - to St. Pat's Cathedral. A long, long way.

Sunday, we visited Malahide Castle, drove through Howth onto a beautiful sandy beach. We gathered shells, filled a bag with sand, and a bottle with water from the Irish Sea to share with family.

I must go back.

To hear the voices singing, laughing, and speaking with love to the little ones. To see the green hills dotted with sheep, the stone fences running every which way making crazy quilt patterns. To see the wild fuchsia, the flower baskets, the multi-colored row houses, the doors. To enjoy the line dried towels, the down comforters.

To feel the strength of 955 young women from the Convent of St. Louis crossing the street after singing at Mass. All in uniform, hair flying, loving life and offering hope for Ireland's tomorrow.

I loved it all.

HarvestFest roots run deep in community

October 10, 1997

I've been a big fan of HarvestFest since 1986, when Louise (Chris) Christensen came around to all the Coupeville shop owners and asked us to enter the chamber's scarecrow contest. We made a pathetic little scarecrow and put it outside the shop.

But not Bonnie Wells of the Sweet Shoppe! Bonnie created a smashing lady of the night with very lumpy legs stuffed into nylons and perched her on top of the bench in front of Joan and DeWayne Hess' "Skipper & Crew."

Neither of us won, but the fun of it made me join the chamber.

Before long, I was crawling around the multipurpose room floor with chairman Estelle Benson taping booth spaces for HarvestFest crafters just as Emily Ramsey, Craig Van Velsor, Irene Thomas and Dorothea Jones and others did when they had the duty.

But HarvestFest started long before any of that. In 1982, chairman Carole Amtmann, with Katie Zimmerman, Mike Putnam and others, created the Squash Festival as a chamber effort — just for fun.

That first year, 300 tickets were sold for a pig roast but when it came time to do the pig in, the hired roaster had disappeared off the face of the earth. There was Lawrence Reuble with a squealing pig in the back of his truck and no one to do the job.

"I was frantic," Carole Amtmann said, "I opened the phone book and jabbed my finger." Amazingly, the person she called knew someone who was able to do the job, and the roast went on. It was a huge success.

Squash Festival was changed to *Squash Bash* in 1986, then to HarvestFest in 1990. The name changed, but the date remained the second weekend in October.

Whatever the name, the participant lists read like the Who's Who of Coupeville. There were two Mother Hubbards, Carol Fraser Davidson and Beth McBrayer, and at least two Kings and Queens of Squash, Ed and Jean Sherman and Freeman and Opal Boyer.

Don Meehan competed in the games — greased squash toss, squash broom chase, squash bowling. Even then, the kids painted and carved Dale Sherman's squash.

In 1986, the main event was the pie throw. Those agreeing to be targets were pelted with whipped cream by many who may have had just a bit of revenge in their hearts.

In line of fire were then-mayor Lew Naddy, sheriff's deputy Murph Cross, attorney Ken Pickard, and teacher Ron Bagby plus

Wayne Tessero, Benye Weber, Cec Stuurmans, Judge Howard Patrick, Sheriff Dick Medina, Carl Ulrich, Mac White, Larry Engle, Virginia Moon and Mike Putnam.

At the end of the day, there was square dancing with Skip Duquette and a great football game between the Coupeville Varsity and the Oak Harbor Sophomores.

In 1989, Christopher Panek, John Stone and John Tristao judged the Squash Bake with Betty Allen counting to see if there really were 1,001 ways to cook squash. In 1991, George Lloyd chaired an Antique Auction, (grandson Rob Workman worked with him). And there was a Barn Dance with the Chuckonotes next to Roy Edenholm's old squash shed when it was an old squash shed.

We've had the best: Sylvia Turkington and the Coupeville Garden Club; Ken Hofkamp, Judy King, the Coupeville Farmers Market, Sno-Isle's Leslie Franzen. At the museum: historians Mickey Clark, Herb Pickard, Lillian Huffstetler, Irene Wanamaker and Larry Thie thanks to Joan Houchen; Help House benefits; and B&B Tours chaired by Marilyn Randock of Old Morris Farm; the banks, the school, and on and on.

Tyee's Sue Hallen chaired HarvestFest for two years after I chaired the 10th year and Fran Einterz the ninth. All that was after Dolores Fresh co-chaired with the creator of it all, Carole Amtmann in 1990.

Great committees and unbelievable support made HarvestFest a community affair ... still is 15 years later. Walk 30 paces anywhere in Coupeville and you will pass a business or a person who has contributed to The Event.

This year, the Girl Scouts have encouraged scarecrow's all around town, Fircrest Tree Farm is bringing trees and apples, there's bratwurst cooking, and the Coupeville Farmers Market has crafts, produce and games.

Outside the high school gym, Lee Roof and Neal Amtmann are sponsoring the Whidbey Island Giant Pumpkin Contest for the second year with prizes for the Ugliest, the Prettiest and in the kid category, the Biggest, and "just maybe a surprise award or two."

You can enter right up to the last minute! Just bring your pumpkin to the weigh-in at 1:00 p.m. on Saturday. "The contest is for fun," Roof says, "and if you win, you have bragging rights for the whole year!"

HarvestFest's a done deal .. a well done deal. See you there!

***

Happy Birthday Jackie Riecks, Val Fuller-Howe, Martha Olsen, and to Cora Bishop a late happy 95th!

Bus ride perfect for people watchers

October 17, 1997

Not too long before we toured Ireland, we took a shorter tour right here on Whidbey Island. We often advise our friends to do the Island on the bus, but we hadn't done it. So one morning we left the Ranger in the Greenbank Park and Ride and we were off.

Although there is no comparison in time or cost - - the whole Whidbey trip only took a few hours and transportation was free - - we found two things exactly the same; the beauty of the land and the friendliness of the people.

Because almost all of our meetings, shopping and dining escapades are north of Greenbank, we took the southbound bus. The plan was to ride to Langley, have breakfast, shop, then head back and stop at Ken's corner for more shopping and lunch.

The south route traveled along back roads with interesting business signs along the way - - a couple I must check out - - and with farms and trees and side roads I didn't remember seeing before.

From the bus, everything looked new and sort of disconnected.

I had a great time. Bus riding is perfect for people watchers. We picked up a dozen or so youths of assorted sizes at different stops who were quietly busy with their own conversations; several adults in uniform were dropped off at their work; Grandma types (I can say that) were met at stops by excited children and relieved moms. I imagined the moms were going to get a break.

And babies were handed off to waiting arms at bus stops by moms or dads then waved at as the bus went on. Non-people watchers boarded wearing ear phones and reading a book and at some secret signal got off with their eyes still glued to their book.

Stepping off the bus in Langley was strange. The door closed, the bus was gone, and there we stood. No base. No nothing. And then freedom set in. No parking space to find, no windows to roll up, no doors to lock, no worry about leaving something behind.

We were all we had.

After breakfast at Mike's Place, we wandered up and down the streets stopping at every shop and art gallery. With no truck to stash purchases in, shopping did become a bit of a quantity control effort. We did fine.

The best part of the trip was that time lost it's power. The bus we had planned to ride to Ken's Corner came and went as did the next one and the next. When we finally did get on board, we just came home. It was dinner time.

We'll do that again. We'll go to Freeland where there are a dozen new shops just waiting to be plundered.

Try the bus. It's a wonderful feeling being foot loose and fancy free.

***

Carol Fraser Davidson called to say she was Mother Hubbard for the first two Squash Festivals - - in 1982 and 1983. She moved to California in 1985 and she's happy to be back living in Coupeville.

Carol has a scrapbook filled with pictures and memorabilia of those early Festivals and offered to share it with me on Sunday at the Uniquely Whidbey Trade Fair.

Somehow, we got our wires crossed and missed each other.

Let's try it again, Carol.

***

Judy Lynn called about HarvestFest too. She said she has pictures of the kings and queens and the Mother Hubbards. Ed and Jean Sherman were king and queen when Carol was Mother Hubbard in 1982, and when she won again in 1983, Karen and Dale Sherman reigned. Beth McBrayer was Mother Hubbard in 1986 when Opal and Freeman Boyer reigned. And in 1987, Andrea Huff was Mother Hubbard and Liz and Dale Sherman king and queen. In 1988, Ann Weaver was the last Mother Hubbard and Don and Debbie Sherman were king and queen.

Judy doesn't know about 1984 and 1985. Do you?

***

Dancers of all ages are promised an eight way bonanza on Nov. 1st. Lovers of square dancing, or Scottish and Irish dancing can learn from the best. Eileen O'Doherty and Erin Raney, both with Northwest Irish Dancers of Seattle, will teach step and Celtic dancing, and Elinor Vandegrift of Royal Scottish Country Dance Society, Seattle Branch will teach you to do like the Scotsmen do.

You can take square dance lessons from Bob Cadwallader and the Whidbey Whirlers, and hula and Middle Eastern dance from experts in those fields. Afternoon classes, (free to $2) begin at noon and are followed with exhibitions. At 8 p.m., take what you learned and dance till 11 p.m.

For specific sites and times read the posters or call the Chamber at 678-5434. A great day and evening for the whole family!!

No lessons for 1970s disco, just DJ Mandolay from LA and $3..dress for it!

Amo content surfing the net these days

October 24, 1997

Mary Amo is one classy lady who knows her mind. She made that clear September 19 in her letter to the editor of *The Coupeville Examiner*.

"Perfect or not," Mary says, "the Growth Management Act has to be implemented NOW." No more fooling around. She wants the county commissioners to act before Whidbey Island looks like Highway 99 in Lynnwood and before we have "an endless procession of strip malls, gas stations, and cookie cutter suburbs." She's asking you to tell our elected commissioners what you want.

Mary knows what she wants. She wants Whidbey to continue to be the greatest place on earth. And she has done her part. An original member of the Greenbank Community Council, she was one of many who took Island Transit and the Department of Transportation by surprise over the Hancock Lake park-and-ride plan.

"We expected this to be an easy project" the DOT project engineer said. "There's a lot more interest here than we expected."

Indeed, there was a lot of interest and Mary kept everyone up to date via the Greenbank homepage on the Internet.

Whidbey is important to her. The Amos came from Ephrata, Washington in 1979 when Clint took early retirement from the Bureau of Reclamation to follow his dream of being a hobby farmer.

Mary, a nurse anesthetist, went back to the UW, earned a degree to become an advance registered nurse practitioner in gerontology. She opened an office on their property and was caring for 25 patients in the early 1980s when Clint had a stroke and had to stop farming.

They made a new plan.

Both were bridge masters. Mary was a director of the American Contract Bridge League, an international organization, since 1960, and Clint was still a fine craftsman. She closed her office and they converted it into what would became the prestigious Greenbank Bridge Studio.

"I called our studio the *Poor Man's Country Club*, there wasn't another place like it anywhere," Mary says. "We worked there together until Clint's death in 1990."

After that, Mary, who had lost one son and was worried about another, a quadriplegic, decided to pack it in and return to Arkansas where she still has family. She went but she couldn't stay. Whidbey Island kept calling her. She returned to Whidbey and continued with the studio until she closed the door early this spring.

"After 15 years in a second career," she says, "I wanted to retire."

That's exactly what Mary has done. Besides her community involvement, she has become a computer nerd.

"I've converted my whole dining area into a computer room, installed skylights and replaced a wall with a picture window so I can look out over the back meadow while I'm on the net."

But she does miss having the bridge group and knows the players are scattered all around the island. "Some people aren't speaking to me anymore," Mary said, "but it will be OK. Someone willing to work really hard can bring it together again, and someone will."

Mary can't, though. She's too busy teaching bridge to Harry in Hawaii and playing on line with Tony Wong in Hong Kong, Jeanette in Mississippi, and Joe Wilson in Alaska. And, every Monday, she and Coupeville's Sylvia Grasser play against whomever. They're called "the Whidbey girls" on the net and are known to be a force to be dealt with.

"You know," she said, "I am the happiest person in the whole world. I get to play, to do whatever I want. I have my privacy, and I have good air. All I need now is Windows '97 - - I have everything else," she said.

She says she's still 45 years old until she starts to do things she did at that age, then her body objects. If it's not physical, she can do it. That works just fine with the Internet. Mary is learning every day from the best. Her current instructor, Internet guru Gary Gordon, is teaching her more and more.

She's doing fine. Take a look at http//www/pioneernet.net/maryamo and see what I mean.

***

I'm told at one time, Cora Bishop played bridge with expert Charles Goren in California!

***

At 7:30 p.m. this Friday, "Artisan," the magnificent a cappella trio from Yorkshire, England appears at CHS Performing Arts Center. Tickets at Coupeville Pharmacy until closing and can be purchased at the high school.

Notice: South Whidbey's singer/actress Shelley Hartle received a call from a friend in Germany last week telling her she had seen "Artisan" in Germany and advised Shelley not to miss their concert.

See you there!

***

The '70s Disco Dance is in the multipurpose room at the Coupeville Elementary School on South Main Street on Nov. 1.

Tartans & Tweeds for sale? Depends on the day

October 24, 1997

One of the oldest and most successful businesses on Coupeville's Front Street, Tartans & Tweeds, might be for sale.

It depends on who you talk to and when.

Katie Zimmerman dreams of retiring."I'm addicted to gardening. That's where I want to be, playing in the dirt."

Carol Amtmann isn't so sure retirement would be that grand. She's vacillating. "Ask me another day," she says, "my answer could be different."

Their husbands are busy, so the partners are on their own. Dale is with the Dispute Resolution program, is a Lion, and raises cattle.Neal builds a mighty fine ice cream cone at Hole in the Wall.

While they may differ on the future focus of their daily lives, it won't change their relationship, which dates back to 1974 at RAF Bicester, England. Their husbands were stationed at Upper Heyford Air Force Base, and the couples met when the Amtmanns moved next door to the Zimmermans.

"There were so many kids in our yard," Katie said, "Carol thought she had moved next to an orphanage, but it was just our four plus a friend or more for each of them."

As friends, their conversations often "headed home." The Zimmermans bragged about the beauty of their "island in the Pacific" and how they had found it easier to visit Seattle area relatives with their youngsters while based at a rented campsite on Whidbey. They also said once they moved to England, they had to buy their very own 10 acres in Greenbank.

The Amtmanns had experience with a Pacific island having visited a booming Mercer Island many times. Zimmermans' island sounded good to them. In the end, Amtmanns beat the Zimmermans to Whidbey by a year. Katie and Dale arrived in May, 1978 and discovered they were in trouble. Their Greenbank property had no buildings. Here they were, with kids and dogs and no place to put them. So, they moved to West Beach, and still live there.

The Greenbank property put the kids through college.

"People often get mixed up on whose kids are whose and even who we are," Carol says. Let's see why. Carol and Katie both have a great sense of humor, and at least one is always in the shop.

The kids, Eric and Wendy went from kindergarten through college together. Both are pilots and captains in the Air Force. Eric in England and Wendy at Fairchild AFB.

Heidi has the dogs, Kris is a new mom in Orting, Washington, and David and John are Zimmermans. There.

For a while, Carol filled in for new mom Cheryl Engle as first grade teacher and later taught at the Central Whidbey Co-op Preschool and Katie was busy raising her boys, but the ladies were ready for something new.

There was a tiny shop in the mall near the Honey Bear called Patrick's Imported Apparel out of Bend, Oregon. When the shop moved into what is now *Ye Kitchen Shoppe* in 1981 and was put up for sale, Katie and Carol bought it and named it *Tartans & Tweeds*.

The story goes that, for 15 years, they kept ordering. More inventory needs more space and before long they filled the entire main floor of the building. "We went to show rooms in Vancouver, Victoria, and San Francisco, where six to eight manufactures from Scotland would take over an entire floor of a hotel to show us what they had," Carol says, "and we'd buy everything."

Katie and Carol were busy in the community too. They created the first Mayfaire and, in 1982, HarvestFest (see The Coupeville Examiner Oct. 10). They are still tickled that the first official duty of Kris Amtmann, the original Mayfair Queen, was to christen the sewage treatment plant with a bottle of Lysol and that Carol Fraser still enjoys remembering being Mother Hubbard.

In 1986, they decided to make money instead of spending it. So they had their kids bring their UW ROTC friends home one weekend and, with their help, moved across the street.

Today, Tartans & Tweeds is a perfect combination of wonderful Scottish and Irish products including capes, shawls, wraps, sweaters, scarves, shirts, and jewelry and beautiful local items.

Stop in Tartans & Tweeds and hear the rest of the story.

***

It's true, former Gov. Booth Gardner visited with friends in Toby's and current Gov. Gary Locke did Front Street last week.

Gary and Mona Lee Locke brought their daughter Emily and a companion to town for lunch. The Lockes spent a relaxed 'touristy' day in Coupeville visiting shops on Front Street, from the Old Town Shop to the wharf. They stopped at Captain's Galley where Shelby served them lunch.

Then there's John, at Penn Cove Antique Mall still blushing over giving his normal parting shot "Be good!" to Gov. Locke and family.

***

Happy Birthday Gordie and KayLynne.

'Generation Gap' benefit this weekend

November 7, 1997

Bennie Rawson and Vern Olsen started this whole thing.

In mid-October, Valerie Wylie and Margie Parker, two school supporters, and yours truly met in the Coupeville music room with Rawson and Olsen.

"Generation Gap," they said, would do a benefit on Nov. 8, only three weeks away.

I wondered if there was time...and then Rawson started talking.

He told us how his students have to juggle space and time every single day; how much they need storage areas for music and safe places for their instruments.

It was easy to see that he cares for the students, the school, the music. Easy to get caught up in his excitement as he talked about how the music department could be improved. "Every musical education facility has specific equipment needs," Rawson said, "and in a multi-use room like Coupeville's, those requirements are essential."

"With just four basic changes," he promised, "our rehearsal area could become much more effective as a place for learning and performing music."

I don't know at what point Bennie Rawson convinced me, but he did. "Imagine our rehearsals." Rawson says, "Every day, five different groups, three bands and two choral groups, rehearse in the Coupeville band room. Every day, we hand out and collect every piece of music we use."

Because there is no proper storage, precious time is wasted every one of those days searching for lost music and missing horn cases.

What's needed? Individual locking instrument storage cabinets to eliminate the daily problems of missing instruments.

Folio Cabinets for both band and choir.

With folio storage, vocalists and instrumentalists would be in charge of their own music. Today, any markings students make on the music are lost to them because it would take entirely too much time for each individual to find his/her music.

Folio storage would solve that problem.

Shelves and Cabinets for organizing and storing sheet music and music equipment.

Even I could see storage space is almost non-existent. Additional storage for instruments and assorted pieces of equipment and supplies is needed.

The remodeling of the present storage units would create two practice rooms. The whole ensemble improves when more advanced students can give one-on-one instruction to less advanced players in a special practice room, the most fundamental part of any music classroom. All four changes are important according to Rawson.

So who is Bennie Rawson?

He and his wife Kimberlie live in Mount Vernon and he just started his second year as the Coupeville Schools Music Director.

Before Coupeville, he taught choir and served as assistant band director in their home town of Cortez, Colorado, and directed the Queen Creek High School band. Kimberlie teaches music in Stanwood and band at the Port Susan Middle School.

Rawson owns and operates Rawson Metal Works, manufacturing music classroom equipment that is distributed nationally through music stores and catalogs. Rawson Metal Works will build all the needed storage units for CHS for just the cost of the materials.

One more thing about Rawson. Monday, I needed 5 minutes of his time. Middle school choir practice was in session and between songs, I entered the room. He gave me his attention and when kids started talking, he turned to them and said, "we have a guest."

And they were silent. Have you been to any classrooms lately? I was impressed.

You know what happens in Coupeville when something has to be done. Especially if it's for our young people. The Coupeville Music Department has needs. Therefore, there's going to be a benefit concert.

The *Generation Gap Swing Band* with big band sounds of the 1930s and '40s offered their talents, Concerts on the Cove is sponsoring the event so every cent goes to specified needs. Gary Shelly printed the tickets for free, CHS band members posted notices, and sold tickets, and five local businesses took the time and made room for ticket sales.

Now it's your turn. Come spend an evening with the *Generation Gap* with the music of Count Basie, Duke Ellington, Benny Goodman and more. The CHS Jazz Band will lead the way this Saturday evening, November 8th at the CHS Performing Arts Center.

It's for our kids.

***

At 8 p.m. on Nov.11, $9 will buy you food for the body and the soul. You can hear Vern and Karl Olsen, Ed Walker, Deborah Lund and the eight other voices of SING!CHRONICITY and eat decadent sweets at the Central Whidbey Chamber of Commerce fund raiser at the Recreation Hall.

'Coupeville Friends' gather to share memories

November 14, 1997

Carol Thrailkill said the "Coupeville Friends" at Rosi's would be ready for pictures by 1 p.m.

Donita, the newspaper's photographer, and I arrived on schedule, but we could have waited an hour or two. They had a lot to talk and laugh about, and they shared some memories with us.

This is the third year the "Coupeville Friends" have met on the island and the first time in Coupeville.

All born to Coupeville families, the 19 women finished school here in the late 1940s, early 1950s. Some left the area for a while and some for good, but most have lived here their entire lives. They wouldn't think of living anywhere else.

Coupeville's Dorothy Clark Keefe, a 1953 graduate with Janice Stoddard Vance and Marge Porter Naval, says the recent gathering was the best ever. "I worked at Whidbey General and couldn't go when they met off island."

Dorothy retired in 1992, and now serves with "Coupeville Friend" Annie Chapman Hesselgrave and Lyla Libbey Snover as town parks and recreation commissioners. The projects they review are close to their hearts: renovation of the Coupeville Recreation Hall and the "Welcome to Coupeville," area near the highway overpass.

Dorothy remembers roller skating in downtown Coupeville on plain old roller skates with Carol Ruthford Thrailkill, whose dad was the town banker.

The bank was in the house at Front and Center where the Vracins now live. The bank was in the front part of the house and the Ruthfords lived in the back.

Lyla Libbey Snover's home was where Coupeville Yarn is now located. "I remember walking home from school in the middle of the street," Lyla recalled, "There wasn't much traffic then, we'd kick our penny loafers ahead of us and when we caught up to them, we'd kick them again."

Lyla met Greenbank's Phil Snover in high school and after they did their time in Japan, while Phil was in the army, they came home to raise their family. In 1965, they built Burgerhaus and operated it for seven years before it was Coupe's Cafe and, now, DJ's.

"It kept the girls off the streets," Lyla laughed, "but it got to be way too much work."

Lyla retired from the post office in Oak Harbor after 14 years and since then she's volunteered wherever she can make a difference: on the town council, town planning commission, Island Transit board, and for Senior Services of Island County.

Eight of the 19 "Friends" came from off Island: Jo Anne Snyder Elbert, Port Ludlow; Gladys Coates Snyder, Olympia; Barbara Ward Johnson, Tacoma; Dolores Elzinga Jacobson, Union; Darlene Ellis Libbey, Burlington; Billie Nelson Smith, Everett; Connie Stevens, Issaquah; and Marge Porter Naval, Kent.

Marilyn Libbey Bailey is active in the Daughters of the Pioneers of Washington; busy gardening and planning a new home, Janice Libbey Coffman is Island County 4-H program co-ordinator; Betty Franzen Jenne volunteers at the sheriff's office; Phyllis Sloth Sherman and her husband Al are involved in the dairy community; and Juanita Gormley Youderian grows raspberries on a farm off Highway 20.

Barbara Morris Stevens, a Realtor who plans to retire this year, said her grandfather built the original Morris farm where her father was raised. In fact, Morris Road was named after her dad's family, Libbey road was named after her mom's family and she married a Patmore. That means Barbara can drive in any direction and be right at home. She skated in Coupeville too, but at the IOOF hall on North Main. (Annie says that building was torn down years ago).

"There was a stage and a beautiful hardwood floor" Barbara said, "perfect for dancing and roller skating."

And then she told me this: Vacant lots along her street were loaded with snakes and Barbara collected the wiggley things to terrorize her mom. Once, Barbara put 16 snakes in her grocery sack and showed them to her mom who was making a pie.

"The ingredients flew all over the kitchen and Mom chased me out of the house and out of the yard and I did what I always did — I headed for Grandma's."

The sack gave out just as she reached Grandma's yard and snakes scattered everywhere sending Barbara's mom home screaming.

"Mom had to promise not to spank me before Grandma let me go home. I was a brat," Barbara admits, "and Grandma spoiled me rotten."

A couple of her cousins agreed.

Living in a small town where everyone knows you can be harsh.

The 'Door' is now wide open in Greenbank

November 21, 1997

Sally Coupe Jacobson was running out the door for supplies when we arrived at *The Green Door Restaurant* Tuesday morning for breakfast, and I didn't catch up with her again till late afternoon.

"I feel like Dorothy in the Wizard of OZ," she said, "but I don't think we're in Kansas anymore!"

Our breakfast was just as Sally and Randy had promised in March, the food was fresh — fresh from the farm and fresh from the sea.

Their philosophy, that running a restaurant is about serving friends, and being real, shows everywhere - - in the warm welcome, the comfortable surroundings, the attention to service. Greenbank's newest restaurant is open daily from 6:30 a.m. 8 p.m. and on Friday and Saturday until 9 p.m.

Congratulations Sally and Randy. It was well worth the wait.

***

We told Shellie she'd love SING!CHRONICITY and that the vocalists, 12 of the finest voices on the island, would blow her away. She came, she heard, they conquered. Why is it certain songs affect us differently when people we know are singing? When they sang *White Christmas*, I was that homesick freshman at St. John's Academy in Jamestown, ND, 300 miles from home and then hearing *Jolly Old St. Nicholas* made me a believer again.

Only unhappy notes of the evening, were the sad sounds of a little boy who is painfully cutting a tooth or two. Have faith, Karl and Deb, Kaj's teething too shall pass.

***

Generation Gap and the Coupeville High School Jazz Band pushed everyone's happy buttons at the benefit for Coupeville Music Department.

While teen-agers Allison and Elizabeth danced in the lobby, the entire audience was in action. The tapping feet, the clapping hands and swaying bodies said it all. By the time director Dick Tilkin invited anyone to "come dance by the stage," Don Lister was already out of his seat. Everyone else stayed put...until the band played *In the Mood*.

That did it! In a flash, Gordie and I were down those steps with the Bronsons right behind us. *In the Mood* is not a tune you tap your feet to. You *have* to dance.

Lister's love of music hasn't changed one iota since we first met. He and Mary Martha Piazzon were just two of the couple dozen people of all ages who danced on the grass at the pavilion to the music of *Rivertalk* a couple summers ago. A self proclaimed "peasant in training," Lister says more people would dance if they didn't think the whole world was watching them.

"The world couldn't care less," says this Englishman, "unless you are having fun, then everyone wants to be part of it."

By George, I think he's right!

***

Beautiful Christmas Crafts are everywhere, but goodies for the holiday are few and far between. St. Mary's Catholic Church Bake sale Saturday from 10 a.m. to 3 p.m., may be the answer.

You might even pick up a treasure or two.

***

Six-year-olds Jason and Jordie spent the weekend with us. Before noon on Saturday, we had swapped bedrooms twice, dug carrots, charged — full speed ahead — to the barn to feed the pony, to Shellie's to feed the goats, walked the foot trail, set a record tearing up and down the deck with the remote controlled car, and played the organ using earphones, thank you.

We took flashlights along when we went to Fort Casey to examine every inch of the ups and downs and ins and outs of each black cavern. They did their best to cheer me up a steel ladder with shouts of "don't look down." OK, so I was only a few steps off the ground but to me each rung is crucial and I was not going one step further. I found another way out.

At noon, we counted on the old tale that eating lunch makes kids sleepy. That's a fallacy. Food fuels the young! After many more hours of non-stop action, we were exhausted and they ate dinner and watched *Cinderella* in their pajamas. Wishful thinking.

Sunday morning was the challenge. Long ago, dressing five little ones by myself wasn't too hard and we were rarely late for church. We weren't late Sunday either, but just getting two ready was a major task.

The rest of the day mirrored Saturday and then they were gone.

I miss them. The house is way too quiet.

Gordie says grandmas are funny.

Perhaps.

Rojas defy the averages to celebrate 25th

November 28, 1997

On November 11, 1972, there were a lot of people worrying about a pair of 19 year olds, Janet Dunn and Manny Rojas.

The couple had just graduated from Coupeville High School the year before and here they were standing before Father Heffernan in St. Mary's Church on Main Street exchanging marriage vows.

Turns out it was a not to worry situation.

Twenty five years later, on November 7, they renewed those vows. Same church, same priest, different attendants.

Standing beside them this time were their children, Celena, 19, who attends North Seattle Community College and Joe, 11, a 6th grader in Coupeville. Janet said she was thrilled to see how excited the kids were about the renewal celebration.

"Nineteen really was young," Janet says, "and today, with everything so different, it's way too young, but in 1972, I was one of the last in my class to marry."

Both Janet and Manny work. He has owned and operated FM Concrete Construction since 1983 and Janet has been a Realtor at Windermere/CIR since 1987.

Although lots of people celebrate their 25th wedding anniversary, it's not as common as it used to be. Raising kids isn't as easy either. Neither Manny or Janet would change a minute of any of it.

The Rojas just returned from spending their second honeymoon in Hawaii on the island of Kauai, which was perfect for them. They've been to Maui, but on Kauai, there were lots of couples just enjoying time together.

"Everything was beautiful. We spent a lot of time smelling the flowers, 'Ferdinand the Bull,' came to mind," Janet laughed.

The Mai Tais weren't too bad either.

I wish more youngsters had been able to see the happiness the Rojas' commitment brought to their family and to an entire community.

An example much needed in today's world.

Congratulations!

***

***

Dropped some mail at the Coupeville Post Office last week.

I have to tell you, it's embarrassing to see a familiar car pull into a disabled parking space and see someone I know hop out and literally run into the building with a single letter or package.

I am fully aware that many debilitating illnesses cannot be seen by the naked eye. I am also fully aware of the importance of that extra space for people with canes or walkers and for loading and unloading a wheel chair.

This holiday season, let's share the wealth.

We have our health, let the sticker bearers have their space.

***

Carol Coble's kids go to two different schools on Maxwelton Road. She takes them every day and wonders why the road crews couldn't take their coffee break between 8:45 a.m. and 9 a.m.

Parents have a terrible time getting in and out of the area with all the moving machinery, she says. "It's hard enough trying to get them to school on time. Ideally, the work should have been done during the summer school vacation, now we need their help."

***

Max Hively, our year round Santa, fully intends to be back on the street soon with his wheel chair loaded with toys for kids.

"Just as soon as I get over being half way lazy, and as soon as my supply gets replenished," he said.

Max said he can't drive his truck anymore because of his medication, "but I can get around in my chair!"

Max could use a couple elves to help him distribute the toys too.

"Just to give me a hand," he says. He is still delivering happiness to those in the VA Hospital in Seattle, so there are many, many who depend on him.

If you have some toys to share with others or could serve as his legs on his trips around town, call Max at 678-7404. He asked me to thank all of his friends. Consider yourselves hugged.

***

Let's make it better this year. Let's change "Don't Drink and Drive" to "Even One Drink, Don't Drive."

***

We have so much to be thankful for again this year. How is it that each one is better than the last?

***

Happy Birthday, Lois - - Happy Anniversary, Beckie and Fred.

Driver is truly an inspiration for kids

December 5, 1997

Mel and June Driver hit the floor running December 3. Their flight to Hawaii left early and they weren't going to miss celebrating the first week of their ninth wedding anniversary on the Big Island or mess up their second week in Kilauea National Park.

The Drivers deserve some sun and fun. They are busy people.

June works part time for a storage company, but because her real love is for the elderly, she understands Mel's passion for volunteering with seventh graders at Coupeville Middle School.

"He has a special way of helping kids be successful."

What do elderly people and successful kids have in common?

Respect, love, and understanding. Mel's desire to see kids succeed started when his mom, Levance, entered Careage of Whidbey in 1991. She was a favorite of the Life Skills class when they visited Careage every other week with director Kay Foss. Levance told the students stories, showered them with love and made them laugh. After her death in 1996, the class sent a sympathy card to the Drivers who let the students how much their visits had meant to his mother.

Then Mel had a stroke. For him, it was a life changing event. He decided he needed to do something special and offered to become a part of the Careage program. He was invited to join and started regular visits not only to Careage but to the classroom and he's been involved in the class Ropes Course, twice.

"I just encourage the kids and serve as a kind of an inspiration. I am 72 years old, you know," he said. Because of his stroke, the directors were worried about his "hands-on" endeavors, but "I told them, when I get tired, I'll sit down." Most of the time, he's much too busy connecting with students, convincing them of their worth and abilities to be concerned about his own health.

Listening to him talk, there is no doubt he is a southern gentleman. Born in Griffin, Georgia, Mel spent a short time in Indiana, then returned to Griffin and lived there until he joined the Navy in 1942. His first tour of duty in Washington state was at Keyport, and after a career that took him to California, NAS Whidbey, and Vietnam, he retired in 1974.

"I decided the best place to raise kids was on Whidbey Island so I brought them back here." One of his children lives in Bellevue, but the rest are back in California.

Mel says the best things he did in the last few years was to "capture and marry June," a military transplant who was ready to return to her native Duluth, Minnesota.

Kay Foss and her class disagree. They think Mel's connection with them is the best. His positive, enthusiastic encouragement has meant a great deal to each of them and they hope he's around for a long, long time.

***

December is a crazy month.

Oh, I know, many of you had your outside lights glowing before Thanksgiving and inside, candles were lit and everything smelled wonderful. Fine. Nothing like that was happening at our house until we learned our California grandbabies were coming for a day or two before we all went to Turkey Day in Portland.

So, something had to be done. Santa and his reindeer were placed on the mantel, the Mighty Christmas Mouse sat comfortably in his chair, the crèche was in place, our Avon drummer and skater were in a ready, set, go, position in the entry, and Little Bear was in his sleigh on the hearth.

After a beautiful Thanksgiving, Mighty Christmas Mouse and Little Bear moved to California to live with KayLynne and Emmy and our house was very quiet...again.

***

Beautiful music is planned at the CHS Performing Arts Center this season. The High School's winter concert 7 p.m. Thurs. Dec. 4, and Middle School's concert is Mon., Dec. 8 at 7 p.m.

***

I spent an hour with Gail Koetje-Neil talking about her *Christmas Celebration in Song* Dec. 6 at 7:30 in CHS Performing Arts Center. "I like to include a student flute accompaniment to *What Child is This?* and *Silent Night* and the whole community and trumpets in the finale *Joy to the World*."

Koetje-Neil's accompanist, Phillip Kelsey, is music administrator and assistant conductor for Seattle Opera. Koetje-Neil, a featured soloist with symphony orchestras, chorales, Broadway musical and opera companies, and a concert recitalist has performed before audiences all over the United States and Europe.

Advance tickets are $10 and available at Coupeville Pharmacy, Wind & Tide Bookshop, The Daily Grind, Book Bay and at Flowers by the Bay. All tickets at the door are $12.

The concert is sponsored by Concerts on the Cove. For info call 678-4684.

Wish you were here

December 12, 1997

It saddens Heidi Cope that her girls, Julie and Kathy have never been held in their grandmothers' arms.

They have never seen her bright smile.

They have never heard her laugh.

When Heidi's boys, Robert and Richard, were babies, their grandmother was there to love them, but they were too young at the time to remember her warmth now.

That wasn't the way it was supposed to be. Because of a drunk driver, though, that's the way it is.

Fredric and Erna Haffer dreamed of a wonderful life in the United States when they emigrated from Bavaria in 1951 with their daughters Heidi, who was almost 11, and Ursel, 7. Fredric had a sister in South Bend, Indiana and a job was waiting there for him.

For the next 13 years, the Haffers were an important part of the South Bend community. Erna sang in the church choir and worked as a furrier. She was famous for her cooking and her pastries were out of this world.

Sunday dinners were a weekly affair and Bavarian holiday traditions were a constant in their home.

They were happy in Indiana, but they missed the mountains of their homeland, so Colorado seemed to be the perfect place for the Haffers to celebrate their 25th wedding anniversary. That was their first vacation alone. By then, Heidi and her husband Adam had two children, and Ursel was 21 and attending college.

Erna and her husband were driving near St. Joseph, Missouri, less than 500 miles from home when a drunk driver changed their lives.

Sandra, a college student, with three friends in her car, tried to pass the Haffers. The girls had been drinking and Sandra couldn't make the pass. The bumpers of the cars hooked. Nothing could stop the disaster.

June 4,1964, Erna, wife of Fredric, mother of Heidi and Ursel, grandmother of Robert, 2 1/2 and Richard, 4 1/2 was dead at the age of 45. About 2,500 people attended her funeral.

One of the girls in Sandra's car was killed. One will never walk again and another was bruised. Sandra was fine.

Ursel and her husband now live in Cleveland, Ohio, and Heidi and her husband settled in Coupeville in 1991.

Erna and Fredric's six grandchildren and six great-grandchildren are being taught the Bavarian traditions by their daughters. They are shown the family albums from the 1800s, and they see family pictures on the wall.

Many of the grandchildren knew Fredric, who lived to be 83, but Erna's stories have to be told to them by Heidi and other family members.

***

Heidi Cope is a member of MADD - - Mothers Against Drunk Drivers.

She knows too well how lives are destroyed when drivers who are under the influence of alcohol and other drugs hit the road.

And she wants to do something about that.

According to Island County Sheriff Mike Hawley, very few roads on Whidbey Island can handle more than two cars, the winding roads make the problem worse, and when drugs, including alcohol, are added to the equation, it can become a nightmare.

In Island County, Hawley said, we are fortunate because our judges sentence drunk drivers to the maximum sentence.

But MADD, with members like Heidi Cope, are working to see that drunk driving laws are toughened, and that the current laws are enforced, throughout the United States.

And they encourage people to tell their legislators that they want stricter laws against drunk driving.

The Island County Chapter of MADD, offers a wealth of information, as well as speakers who will go to schools and workplaces to educate others about the dangers of drunk driving.

And what about ordinary people who attend holiday parties where alcohol drinks are served?

Designate a driver.

Community comes together to help one of its own

December 19, 1997

Jim Davis was worried that his thinking wasn't up to par when I talked to him Monday. He hasn't been able to sleep well, but he knows that's a normal problem after surgery. He said he's feeling better every day.

Jim started having problems earlier this year and in October he had an MRI. The test disclosed a tumor on his brain, and on December 3, he entered Swedish Hospital in Seattle. The tumor was malignant and most of it could be removed. Some couldn't, and it's the kind of tumor that has a habit of regrowing.

They'll have to watch that. He'll have radiation treatments for six weeks, five days a week.

Jim says he's healthy from the neck down, but his life has changed completely. What he does and how he thinks about things is a lot different since the surgery. Adjusting to those changes hasn't been easy. One thing he knows for sure, he's grateful he lives in such an amazing community.

A community full of loving, caring people. "People have done such wonderful things for us," he said, "I am humbled."

The community isn't finished yet. As always, islanders are quick to come together when one of their own needs help. Jim and Carolyn have no insurance, and surgery and radiation treatments cost big bucks. So, at 7:30 p.m. Saturday, December 27, a benefit is planned for the Davises at the Coupeville High School Performing Arts Center. Local musical groups will offer their best including *SING!CHRONICITY*, the *Shifty Sailors*, *Maggie and the Older Boys*, and members of the *Saratoga Chamber Players*. Vern Olsen and Roxallanne Medley promise a surprising duet.

Items for an auction of wonderful items from island businesses are being gathered by Mendy McLean-Stone and Kermit Chamberlin. Items collected so far include a ride on John Stone's Cutty Sark and Roger Purdue prints from Susan Berta's WSU crowd.

WSU is also in charge of the concessions. Apple deserts are requested, but anything delicious will be gladly accepted.

Tickets are available at the Wind and Tide Bookshop in Oak Harbor, Whidbey Stationers in both Oak Harbor & Freeland and at the Coupeville Pharmacy.

Jim, a long time Whidbey Island resident, was six when his parents moved to the island in 1942. He graduated from Coupeville High School in 1955 then worked in Tacoma for a few years.

That's where he met and married Carolyn in 1968. Together they operate the Fircrest Tree Farm on Houston Road.

Jim and Carolyn Davis didn't plan to start a business in the early 1970s when they moved into the house his father built in 1947. Most of the trees on the property had been logged before their time and they wanted to replace them, so they planted a few hundred seedlings.

By 1973, so many people were placing orders for trees they established the Fircrest Tree Farm. They offer plants and shrubs and a variety of trees and have an apple orchard. Their daughter Denise is in charge of the flowers.

In addition to Denise, who lives in Clinton, the Davises have five other children, James L. III in Freeland, David in San Jose, Laura in Lake City, Carol in Arlington, Robin in Everett and Lisa in Lake Stevens. They also have five grandchildren. One of them, Doneen, lives with them so she can attend CHS, her favorite school.

Jim and Carolyn are active in groups interested in preserving as much of our beautiful island as long as possible so those who follow will be able to enjoy it too.

"We all have a stake in trying to stay in balance so we can keep a bit of this Eden we've grown up around and still have a reasonable portion in a development mode," Jim said.

He says he's learned a lot serving on committees. He's willing to agree to disagree and sees the value of respecting the ideas of opponents without giving up or selling out.

They are both involved in the South Whidbey Tilth Organization and the island Chapter of the Rhododendron Society.

Jim is chairman of the Agricultural Advisory Committee for the Greenbank Farm Management Group, and was involved in preparation of the draft for the comprehensive plan of the Whidbey Agriculture Forest Council for Land Use Policy. He's a member of the Heritage Lands Committee, and the Whidbey/Camano Land Trust and Policies Committee. He also served on the Ground Water Management Study board, and from 1987-1991 on the Coupeville School Board.

This man has given so much to the community and now he needs our help. All proceeds will go toward defraying his medical expenses.

A "Davis Benefit Fund" has been established at InterWest Savings Bank.

Call 678-3687 if you can help with food, time or talent.

See you the 27th!

Searching for the best way to say 'thank you'

January 30, 1998

Gordie came home January 20. His walker is standing idle and no way will he use the cane.

He does just fine on his own.

He still beats me at rummy, he's reading again, and works a bit on the computer, but 39 days of being so very ill has taken its toll. He's 30 pounds lighter and speaks ever so softly.

Gordie had a brain stem stroke on December 13, and thanks to Lori and Jack Miller, he made it to Whidbey General in time.

Following 10 days of excellent care by Doctors Roof and Long, he was sent to Northwest Stroke Rehab Center in Seattle. Within hours he was found to have pneumonia and transferred to ICU at Northwest Hospital and spent the next eleven days fighting for his life.

Later, he was in the Special Care Unit and the Transitional Care Unit for a while, and finally back to the rehab center. He hasn't learned to swallow yet.

He will.

Since the beginning, I've limited this column to 700 words. Sometimes I get carried away, but most are pretty close.

Good thing. It would take most of the paper to thank all of you who visited Gordie at the hospitals, brought flowers, sent encouraging words via e-mail and card after card and called and called again.

Our "personal secretary" was always full.

It would also take the entire paper to list all of you who are still offering help and those who already have. I was picked up at the ferry late one night. Our mail was collected day after day after day, and over and over, beautifully wrapped offerings of nourishment appeared at our door.

I was even treated to the last two sandbakkels of the season just because I said they reminded me of home.

And to top it all off, *The Examiner* didn't cut my salary a single dime!

We've learned a couple things during this time.

We know now, that some nurses, male or female, were born to nurture and some were not, that we chose the right doctors, and that both Whidbey General and Northwest have kind, caring, efficient staffs.

We know that trips should never be delayed.

We've learned that with our kids and grandkids beside us, we can conquer the world.

Eleven of our children were here; three of them, plus a spouse, a grandson and granddaughter flew in from California. Our Portland daughter and spouse drove back and forth. Shellie and both of her Randys supported the ferry system. Rob wheeled his chair right up to Gordie's bedside more than once, and those who live in the Seattle area were in and out of Northwest daily from beginning to end.

Except when they made me go home with them to rest.

I learned sleeping over isn't as much fun as it was when I was a kid, but found the beds at both Heidi's and Rick's much more comfortable than hospital cots. And the pampering was terrific!

Too many times in the last month, the words "thank you" have sounded so weak. Two of my sisters are also searching for a better word, one for all of the people who attended her husband's funeral, and the other for the outpouring of good wishes for her recovery from radical surgery.

It's hard. I still remember our feeling of inadequacy in writing the letter of thanks to the editor after Rob's accident.

How does one describe so much gratitude? I think Jim Davis used the right word, he said he felt "humbled."

Humbled.

Yes, that's the word we've been trying to find. It fits.

'Backstage' crew comes together for music students

February 6, 1998

Whenever two groups with a common goal come together, everything goes much more smoothly.

In November, Coupeville School Board member Valerie Wiley and teacher's aid Margie Parker were the only parents planning the benefit for the school district's music department along with band director Bennie Rawson and Concerts on the Cove.

Valerie and Margie knocked themselves out getting volunteers to help. A couple months later, Troy and Anne Kostek worked hard to create a newsletter to make parents aware of the needs of all middle and high school performing arts students.

The two groups came together in December and formed *"Backstage,"* an independent nonprofit organization, with a temporary board of dedicated parents.

The goal of "Backstage" is to improve lighting and sound in the performing arts center, buy uniforms for the middle and high school bands, and raise money for trips to band competitions, festivals, choir contests, and drama productions.

Anne Kostek is president of "Backstage," Charles Skow is treasurer and Cathy Mitchell, secretary. Meetings are held on the second Wednesday of each month in the music room of the high school. Currently, there are 12 members of "Backstage," but all members of the community, including high school students, are invited to join them on February 11. If you don't need "one more meeting," support the cause in your own way. Coupeville's Cheyenne Business Equipment is donating paper and copying costs for the current issue of the newsletter.

Because they joined forces, the February 21 benefit will be much easier for Concerts on the Cove to sponsor. And what an event it will be. The Performing Arts Center, decked out with little round tables on the huge dance floor, will be filled with the best swing music performed by the "Sea Notes" under the direction of Bruce Seltveit.The benefit is 10-7 p.m. Saturday, Feb. 21. Adults $10, students $3.

If you haven't been out dancing for awhile, you had better shape up, because the 20 couples taking lessons through Community Education classes will probably be showing off their new talent at the benefit. Although Gordie and I have been known to cut a mean rug now and then, this time we'll pass.

You do it. For the kids.

***

I have to tell you something I hope you never need to know.

If I were the only one who went through this nightmare, I wouldn't say a word, but there are three other women in Central Whidbey who tell me they suffered the same experience with their loved one.

When Gordie was in the hospital, very, very ill, he developed what the hospital staff explained away as "ICUitis."

Because of the need for regular medications, blood withdrawals, checks for vital signs and shift change checks, nurses were in and out of his room constantly.

Each procedure was done by a different person at a different time. Sleep deprivation became a major problem. For Gordie, fear, delusions, and paranoia set in, and every nurse, doctor, every person who entered the room was perceived as a threat

When I arrived at 6:30 one morning, Gordie told me he knew there was a plot to do away with him. But he had a plan. I would park the Ranger by the front door and we would make a run for it.

Because I didn't know what was happening, - - didn't know anything about "ICUitis," I tried to reason with him. I explained to him that the staff just wanted to make him well.

I immediately became the enemy in Gordie's mind. I had been brainwashed.

His anger and devastation at what he saw as my betrayal lasted only a few hours, but had I known it could happen, I would have handled it differently. I don't know how, but at least it would have been easier.

Now you know. May you never have to remember what I just told you.

By the way, at one point, Gordie tried to organize the nurses.

Surprised?

He wanted them to work in teams, several of them doing their thing at the same time, so he could get some rest.

***

The candy tuft is blooming, the crocuses are ready to open, and sitting on the deck early in the morning is wonderful. Isn't it nice to have something happening that you didn't do and don't have to do anything about?

It's so good to be back.

Club celebrates 50 years of blooming success

February 13, 1998

"A gardener is someone who believes what goes down, must come up."

No one knows who said that, but members of the Greenbank Garden Club understand it. They've been heeding those words and reaping the rewards for 50 years.

The Greenbank Garden Club's spring and fall plant sales are events to behold.

Both start at 10 am, but the line of wanna-be gardeners begins to form at least an hour earlier.

It's a mixed blessing. Not only is it possible to be windblown and soaking wet by opening time, but choice plants will still be on the tables and there's time to visit with friends not seen since the last sale.

Come for the spring sale Saturday, April 18, and come early.

***

Originally part of the Evergreen District, the Greenbank Club is now on its own and can spend its time and money on projects of its members' choice.

They are a busy group. The club awards 4-H scholarships so that youths can participate in the Island County Fair. It keeps Smugglers Cove clear of litter. Good Cheer is helped through food drives. This year, a case of crayons was donated to Help House clients, and the club contributed to the Jim Davis Fund.

Members volunteer at Meerkerk Gardens and do the Greenbank Farm front walk, which they also decorated for Christmas. They have planted a zillion tulips for spring.

Money earned in 1998 will be used in the community in honor of those who founded the club.Organized in 1948 by 14 women, the Greenbank Garden Club now has 40 members — five of them are men.

"We've been up and down in membership over the years," said long time member Peggy Berg. "In the beginning, we met in homes, but as more people joined, we started meeting in the Progressive Club building on the first Thursday of each month, and still do."

Over time, the focus of the club changed from the pioneer women's dirt projects to floral design. Today, both subjects are equally important with lectures on soil amendment, planting and harvesting as well as arranging beautiful centerpieces.

The February meeting of the Greenbank Garden Club was a tribute to charter members of and to the club's achievements.

Betty Engstrom, one of the original 14, was the special guest. Yearbooks, dating back to 1949, with pictures, cards and newspaper articles telling the history of the group, were enjoyed and selected parts read by current officers.

This year, the books are in Annie Horton's care.

As corresponding secretary, Annie read then-secretary Edith Magnuson's minutes of the 1953 Christmas Party. It holds a special place in her heart. She was six months old when Edith wrote those words and today, Annie and Ross live in the old Magnuson House off Highway 525.

***

Happy Valentine's Day!!

This & That, Part 2, with more stories of the wonderful people, places and things of Central Whidbey Island, will be published in late 1999.

This & That, Part 2 is being written one column at a time, and published each Friday in The Coupeville Examiner.